Poverty and
social exclusion
in Britain

David Gordon, Ruth Levitas, Christina Pantazis, Demi Patsios, Sarah Payne, Peter Townsend
Townsend Centre for International Poverty Research, University of Bristol

Laura Adelman, Karl Ashworth, Sue Middleton
Centre for Research in Social Policy, Loughborough University

Jonathan Bradshaw, Julie Williams
Social Policy Research Unit, University of York

JR
JOSEPH
ROWNTREE
FOUNDATION

The Joseph Rowntree Foundation has supported this
project as part of its programme of research and
development projects, which it hopes will be of value
to policy makers, practitioners and service users. The
facts presented and views expressed in this report,
however, are those of the authors and not necessarily
those of the Foundation.

Published by
Joseph Rowntree Foundation
The Homestead
40 Water End
York   YO30 6WP
www.jrf.org.uk

ISBN 1 85935 059 3

Price £15.95

Designed by Adkins Design
Printed by Fretwells Ltd

Printed on recycled paper

Contents

Acknowledgements

The Poverty and Social Exclusion Survey of Britain (PSE) was undertaken by the Office for National Statistics in 1999 as a follow-up survey of a sample of respondents to the 1998/99 General Household Survey. The questionnaire was derived from a review of the best social surveys from around the world. It builds on over one hundred years of experience in the social sciences in Britain in the scientific study of poverty. The authors acknowledge the contribution made to this research from the following sources and surveys:

Breadline Britain in the 1990s, British Crime Survey, British Household Panel Survey, British Social Attitudes, Canadian General Social Survey, Disability Discrimination Act Baseline Survey, Eurobarometer, European Community Household Panel Survey, EuroQol 5D, General Household Survey, GHQ12, Harmonised Question Set, Health Survey of England, Living in Ireland Survey, Living in Britain Survey, Lorraine Panel Survey, MORI Omnibus, Poor Wales, Poverty in the United Kingdom, Small Fortunes: National Survey of the Lifestyles and Living Standards of Children, Survey of English Housing and the Swedish Living Conditions Survey.

The survey, Breadline Britain in the 1990s, was funded by London Weekend Television (LWT) with additional funding from the Joseph Rowntree Foundation and was carried out by Marketing and Opinion Research International (MORI). It was conceived and designed by Joanna Mack and Stewart Lansley for Domino Films, with the help of Brian Gosschalk of MORI.

We would like to thank Björn Halleröd of the University of Umeå, Tony Manners, Dave Elliot, Linda Murgatroyd, Jo Maher, Ann Bridgwood, Olwen Rowlands and June Bowman at the Office for National Statistics, Richard Berthoud and Jonathan Gershuny at the University of Essex, Rick Davies of Swansea University and Michael Bitman at the University of New South Wales for their helpful advice. We would also like to thank Brian Gosschalk, Mark Speed and Sarah Birtles from MORI for their helpful comments and their work on the preparatory stages of this research. We would like to thank Roger Bullock for making the facilities of the Dartington Social Research Unit available.

Helen Anderson edited, typed and formatted the original manuscript.

We would like to thank Barbara Ballard and Dominic Hurley from the Joseph Rowntree Foundation for their advice, encouragement and support throughout this project and Donald Hirsch for his editing work. Finally, we would like to thank the members of the Advisory Committee for their helpful support.

The following authors contributed to this report:
Chapter 1 - Peter Townsend and David Gordon;
Chapter 2 - Jonathan Bradshaw and Julie Williams;
Chapter 3 - Laura Adelman, Karl Ashworth and Sue Middleton;
Chapter 4 - David Gordon;
Chapter 5 - Ruth Levitas, Christina Pantanzis, Demi Patsios and Peter Townsend.

Foreword

This report presents the initial findings from the most comprehensive survey of poverty and social exclusion ever undertaken in Britain. The study was undertaken by researchers at four universities and the fieldwork was conducted during 1999 by the Office for National Statistics. The main part of the fieldwork, conducted during September/October 1999, was a follow-up survey of a sub-sample of respondents to the 1998/99 General Household Survey.

It is particularly important at this time to create a base line understanding of the nature of poverty and social exclusion. On any measure, poverty at the turn of the new millennium remains one of the greatest social problems challenging Britain, and reducing social exclusion is at the heart of Government policy. The current Government has declared its determination to eradicate child poverty, and the UK has an international commitment substantially to reduce poverty over the coming years. We very much hope that the Office for National Statistics will be able to use the approach of this project in future surveys to measure progress in these areas.

The method used in this survey echoes, but extends, the approach used in the Breadline Britain Surveys of 1983 and 1990. This survey measures poverty in terms of deprivation from goods, services and activities which the majority of the population defines as being the necessities of modern life. Income and employment data are incomplete proxies for measuring poverty and inclusion and policy-makers will need to be cautious in their interpretation.

The data in this study will add immeasurably to our understanding of the nature of poverty and social exclusion in Britain. We hope that measuring deprivation in this way will also get us beyond the sterile arguments about whether we should be concerned with absolute or relative poverty. This is an absolute measure in the sense that it is concerned with the possession or otherwise of particular goods and services, but it is relative in the sense that the goods and services included reflect the population's judgement on what it is essential to have in Britain today.

Clearly we need to get beyond arguments about definitions and into understandings of the nature of poverty and deprivation that can contribute to better policies. This study begins this process. It shows that the proportion of households living in poverty in terms of both low income and multiple deprivation of necessities has increased from 14 per cent in 1983 to 21 per cent in 1990 to over 24 per cent in 1999. Thus about a quarter of people in Britain are deprived on this measure, despite the huge increase in affluence seen over the last two decades.

There is a great deal of data to be mined from this survey, including, but going beyond that contained in this report. This data can inform policies aimed at reducing the extent of poverty and social exclusion. Further working papers and a book will be produced by the project team over the coming months and we hope that others will also use the rich information that is available.

Sir Peter Barclay
Chair, Joseph Rowntree Foundation

① Introduction

The present British Government is committed to tackling poverty, and to abolishing child poverty in 20 years.[1] If they are to succeed in these objectives then good and up-to-date research on poverty and social exclusion, as well as more exact measures of trends and causes, is required. Unfortunately, in the last 20 years there has been very little such research. The research that forms the basis of this report is intended to serve three purposes:

- to re-establish the long national tradition of investigating and measuring the scale and severity of poverty;

- to extend this tradition to the modern investigation of social exclusion so that for the first time the relationship between poverty and social exclusion can be examined in depth;

- to contribute to the cross-national investigation of these phenomena, as Britain agreed to do at the World Summit for Social Development in 1995 (UN, 1995).

In 1998 and 1999, a team from four universities joined with the Office for National Statistics to undertake a survey of poverty and social exclusion, using data from the government's General Household Survey (GHS) and from its Omnibus Survey, and interviewing in more detail a sub-sample of the GHS. This major investigation originated as a follow-up of two earlier surveys of Breadline Britain,[2] which measured the number of people who were poor in terms of being unable to afford items that the majority of the general public considered to be basic necessities of life. The new survey used a similar method to measure poverty in terms of socially perceived necessities and added questions relating to other measures of poverty and also to

social exclusion. The new survey is called the Poverty and Social Exclusion Survey of Britain (PSE). Its results show how both the perception of necessities and the level of poverty have evolved in the last 20 years. It starts to develop ways of measuring social exclusion, and also includes measures that are compatible with international standards for measuring poverty.

This introductory chapter discusses the context of the PSE survey: the current levels of poverty in Britain, the ways in which poverty is defined, and the ways it can be measured. It then gives an overview of the approach taken in this survey. The following chapters look at four principal features of the results:

- the number of adults who are living in poverty, and some of their characteristics (Chapter 2);

- the number of children who are living in poverty, their characteristics and those of their households (Chapter 3);

- trends over time in poverty among children and adults (Chapter 4);

- the number of people who are socially excluded according to various measures (Chapter 5).

Chapter 6 summarises and draws conclusions from these findings.

The PSE survey has provided a wealth of new data and many working papers have been written and are still being prepared. This report is an initial analysis to put the main headline results and conclusions from the work into the public domain. A full list of working papers is in Appendix 5.

Current poverty levels according to published government data

The levels of both adult and childhood poverty in relative terms in the UK grew during the 1980s and 1990s, reflecting the growth of inequality of income which was "exceptional compared with international trends" (Hills, 1998, p5). The latest figures show that there were 14.3 million people in the UK living in households with less than half average household income in 1998-9 (see Figure 1). This represented a threefold increase in both the number and the proportion of people in relative poverty between 1979 and 1998-9 (DSS, 2000). The number of children in households at below half average income had grown from 1.4m to 4.4m and, by the mid-1990s, the UK's child poverty rate was the third highest of the 25 nations for whom information was available (see, for example, Bradshaw, 1999; Bradbury and Jantii, 1999; Piachaud and Sutherland, 2000; UNICEF, 2000).

The change, relative to average household income, has been pronounced at the top as well as at the bottom of the income scale. Between 1979 and 1994-5, the incomes of the richest tenth of the population grew by 68 per cent, while those of the poorest grew only 10 per cent, before housing costs, and fell 8 per cent after housing costs (Hills, 1998, p5; see also Hills, 1995 and 1996).

In the first two years of the new Government (1997-8 and 1998-9), the disposable incomes of the poorest and richest decile groups were still edging apart (CSO and ONS, 1996-7, 1997-8 and 1998-9, Table 8.3 and see also similar data for quintiles in ONS 1998, 1999 and 2000). Neither the total number of people nor the number of children living in households with below half average incomes changed significantly between 1996-7 and 1997-8 (Howarth et al., 1999, pp12, 26). However, the number of children increased slightly from 4.4 to 4.5 million between 1997-8 and 1998-9 (DSS, 2000, p199). Evidence of the arrest or reversal of the divergent trend, while eagerly awaited, is not yet showing up in published survey data.

How poverty is defined and measured

Definitions of poverty

The picture of poverty presented above is based only on one possible definition: the number of people with incomes below an arbitrary percentage of the average. The definition is convenient to governments and international agencies because it is fairly easy to estimate in several countries. However, as explained below, it is not scientifically based: that is, it is not based on independent criteria of deprivation or disadvantage; it does not relate to the needs of individuals, or to any agreed definition of

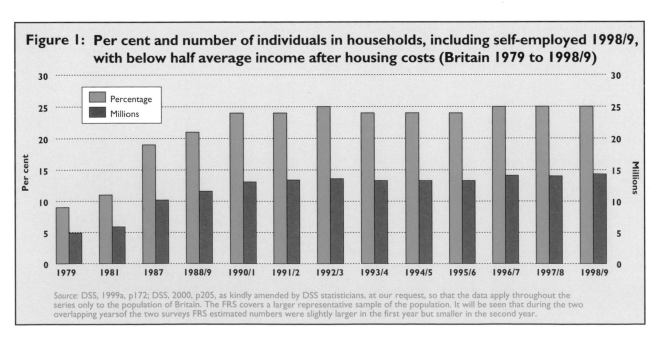

Figure 1: Per cent and number of individuals in households, including self-employed 1998/9, with below half average income after housing costs (Britain 1979 to 1998/9)

Source: DSS, 1999a, p172; DSS, 2000, p205, as kindly amended by DSS statisticians, at our request, so that the data apply throughout the series only to the population of Britain. The FRS covers a larger representative sample of the population. It will be seen that during the two overlapping yearsof the two surveys FRS estimated numbers were slightly larger in the first year but smaller in the second year.

what it is to be poor. As in the cases of radiation, different forms of pollution and global warming, there is a real need to develop acceptable thresholds that lead to significant increases in risk or harm. The income threshold for different types of household that marks the 'poverty line' thus needs to identify income levels, below which there is a statistically enhanced risk of incurring multiple forms of deprivation. The PSE survey attempts to do this. It also asked questions relating to the internationally agreed UN definitions of poverty as shown in the box below.

International definitions of poverty

Many research studies of poverty throughout the twentieth century illustrate an ongoing struggle to extricate the concept of poverty from political ideology and to widen scientific perspectives from narrow concern with the physical and nutritional needs of human beings to include their complex social needs. Part of that struggle has been to find measures by which to compare conditions in different countries, and especially conditions in rich and poor countries, so that priorities might be more securely established.

At the political level, there is some movement towards agreed definitions of poverty across countries. The United Kingdom has no official definition, and Ministers often define poverty in terms of "knowing it when they see it". But the Government has signed treaties and agreements at the European level that define poverty in terms of having insufficient resources to participate in a "minimum acceptable way of life" (EEC, 1981, 1985), even though the EU has reverted on occasions to the relative income standard – that is, the number and percentage of population with less than half, or a smaller or larger fraction of, average household income.[3]

An international agreement at the Copenhagen World Summit on Social Development in 1995 was something of a breakthrough. By recommending a two-tier measure of 'absolute' and 'overall' poverty to be applied to every country, a means was found of bringing all governments together in common purpose. An opportunity was created of exploring the severity of poverty according to standards that seemed to be acceptable everywhere. Even countries where it was assumed absolute poverty no longer existed found it easier to accept an international two-tier approach that self-evidently included their own conditions.

After the Copenhagen summit in 1995, 117 countries including the UK committed themselves to eradicating 'absolute' and reducing 'overall' poverty and to drawing up national poverty-alleviation plans (UN, 1995). Absolute poverty is defined in terms of severe deprivation of basic human needs. Overall poverty is a wider measure, including not just lack of access to basics but also lack of participation in decision-making and in civil and to social and cultural life:

Absolute poverty:

"a condition characterised by severe deprivation of basic human needs, including food, safe drinking water, sanitation facilities, health, shelter, education and information. It depends not only on income but also on access to services." (UN, 1995, p57)

Overall poverty can take various forms including:

"lack of income and productive resources to ensure sustainable livelihoods; hunger and malnutrition; ill health; limited or lack of access to education and other basic services; increased morbidity and mortality from illness; homelessness and inadequate housing; unsafe environments and social discrimination and exclusion. It is also characterised by lack of participation in decision-making and in civil, social and cultural life. It occurs in all countries: as mass poverty in many developing countries, pockets of poverty amid wealth in developed countries, loss of livelihoods as a result of economic recession, sudden poverty as a result of disaster or conflict, the poverty of low-wage workers, and the utter destitution of people who fall outside family support systems, social institutions and safety nets." (ibid., p57)

Operationalising the definitions: measuring poverty
There are a variety of approaches to measuring poverty, outlined in Appendix 1. Simple measures of poverty look only at *relative income*, but agreed international definitions of poverty described in the box on page 9 relate not just to how much money people have, but to whether it is enough for them to maintain a minimum acceptable way of life. Cash income is a key factor, but is not the only indicator of people's access to goods and services. For example, possession of certain kinds of assets is equivalent to additional income; by adding to people's resources, it raises their living standards and their access to goods and services. *Budget standards*, defining the income needed to buy a basket of basic goods, have a closer relationship to the ability of people to purchase basic items. However, they do not encompass all elements that comprise a standard of living. Two ways of measuring low standards of living are by looking at *consumption expenditure* or using *deprivation indices*, based on items that people are deprived of because they cannot afford them. The latter are more accurate, since they give a broader picture than simply what is being spent on consumer goods at a moment in time, and it is this approach that the PSE survey takes.

The PSE survey (described in the following section) makes major use of income data from the GHS but measures poverty in terms of both deprivation and income level: whether people lack items that the majority of the population perceive to be necessities, and whether they have incomes too low to afford them. As well as measuring poverty in these two ways, the survey collected data relating to the UN definitions of poverty as described in the box on page 9 and data that can help assess whether individuals are socially excluded. The report thus brings together information using a variety of poverty measures, but its main data are derived from the investigation of socially perceived necessities.

The 1999 Poverty and Social Exclusion Survey of Britain (PSE survey)

The research was designed initially to replicate two previous national surveys - known as the Breadline Britain surveys – which had been carried out in 1983 and 1990 (Mack and Lansley, 1985; Gordon and Pantazis, 1997). The 1999 PSE survey uses comparable methods based on identifying the items that a majority of the population perceive as necessary, so that the trends spanning nearly two decades can be described and analysed. How the survey approached the measurement of poverty on this basis is outlined in the box below.

The PSE survey approach to measuring poverty

The survey's main task was to produce a measure of poverty based on socially perceived necessities and a scientific definition of deprivation.

This was achieved in three steps, which combined social consensus in determining what should be considered as necessities with scientific methods of using this information to define poverty.

First, a representative sample of the public were asked to indicate which items in a long list of ordinary household goods and activities they thought were necessities that no household or family should be without in British society.

Second, a representative sample were asked which items they already had and which they wanted but could not afford. Items defined as necessities by more than 50 per cent of the population but which were lacked because of a shortage of money were then used to determine deprivation.

Third, a poverty threshold was calculated. The theoretical approach is summarised in Figure 2. Here, individuals are scattered on the chart according to their levels of income and living standard (which can be thought of as the converse to the level of deprivation). This is illustrated in Figure 2 by a cluster of individuals with high levels of both and a cluster with low levels of both. Fewer individuals have a high standard of living and a low income (i.e. top left of Figure 2) and few have a high income and low standard of living (i.e. bottom right of Figure 2). The optimum poverty threshold is set where statistically it maximises the differences between 'poor' and 'not poor', and minimises the differences within these groups. This involved looking at people's incomes as well as their deprivation levels. Figure 2 thus illustrates how this approach aims to identify poverty as a scientific phenomenon rather than just drawing an arbitrary line.

The methodology thus combines a representative popular basis for agreeing what are necessities, with a scientific basis for establishing a level of poverty. Appendix 2 sets out precisely how information on

whether people can afford socially perceived necessities, together with information about their incomes, was used to calculate a poverty threshold. This is a particularly powerful approach because:

- it incorporates the views of members of the public, rather than judgements by social scientists, about necessary items; and

- the level of deprivation that constitutes poverty is based on a scientific calculation, not an arbitrary decision.

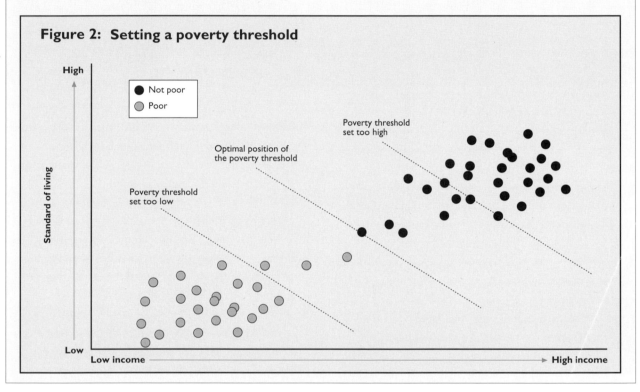

Figure 2: Setting a poverty threshold

In addition to this, the survey did two other things.

It used a measure of *subjectively assessed poverty* to estimate how much money would be needed to avoid absolute and overall poverty as defined at the Copenhagen summit (see above). This involved asking people what they considered to be the minimum income enabling them to rise above these two poverty levels and whether their own incomes exceeded these levels.

The survey also made an attempt to measure *social exclusion*. An extensive programme of development work was supported by the Joseph Rowntree Foundation that included reviews of the available

literature and instruments for measuring both poverty and social exclusion. In addition, a series of group discussions were held to:

- explore how people defined poverty and social exclusion;

- develop and test new indicators of poverty and social exclusion.

As discussed in Chapter 5, social exclusion was looked at in four dimensions – impoverishment, labour market exclusion, service exclusion, and exclusion from social relations. By putting considerable emphasis on social relations and social participation, the survey differs from most analysis, which has focused on low income, lack of work and area deprivation. This has largely been necessitated by a lack of data on social relations. The PSE survey provides an unprecedented opportunity to look at social isolation and lack of participation, which may correlate with or be caused by low income, non-engagement in the labour market and service exclusion, but is not defined by these. The preliminary analysis presented in this report looks separately at each of the four dimensions of social exclusion; future analysis will look at the correlation between different dimensions.

Notes

1   See, for example, the Prime Minister's Beveridge Lecture on 18 March 1999 (Blair, 1999). In the 1999 pre-budget report, the Chancellor of the Exchequer announced the Government's aim to halve child poverty "by the end of the next decade".

2   The first of these surveys was called "Poor Britain" and the second "Breadline Britain" but their similarity has led to them being referred to collectively as the Breadline Britain surveys.

3   In 1975, the Council of Europe adopted a relative definition of poverty as: "individuals or families whose resources are so small as to exclude them from the minimum acceptable way of life of the Member State in which they live" (EEC, 1981). The concept of 'resources' was defined as: "goods, cash income, plus services from public and private resources" (EEC, 1981). On 19 December 1984, the European Commission extended the definition: "the poor shall be taken to mean persons, families and groups of persons whose resources (material, cultural and social) are so limited as to exclude them from the minimum acceptable way of life in the Member State in which they live" (EEC, 1985). According to UNICEF, this definition "is today the most commonly used definition in the industrialised world" though "for practical purposes" it is usually interpreted as "those whose incomes fall below half of average income" (UNICEF, 2000, p6).

Data collection

The research was carried out jointly by a group of researchers from four universities (York, Bristol, Loughborough and Heriot-Watt) and the Office for National Statistics (ONS). It used three sets of data:

1   The General Household Survey (GHS) of 1998-9 provided income and socio-demographic data and the basis for selecting participants in (3) below.

2   The ONS Omnibus Survey of June 1999 included questions designed as part of this survey, asking members of the public about items they considered to be necessities.

3   A follow-up sub-sample survey of the GHS in September/October 1999 looked at how many people cannot afford the items identified as necessities and also looked at both poverty and social exclusion in greater depth.

In developing the survey, some of the new and revised questions were also piloted in a regular omnibus survey carried out by MORI in July 1998. A full report of the development work can be found in Bradshaw et al., 1998.

Appendix 4 gives further details of the data collection methodology. This combination of sources brought together an unprecedented level of information on a nationally representative population in a single data set.

② Adult poverty in Britain

How many adults in Britain are poor and what are their characteristics? This chapter answers this question mainly by assessing who can be defined as poor based on whether they can afford socially perceived necessities. In the final section, it also looks at how many people define themselves as poor.

The analysis starts off, in the following section, by looking at how many adults cannot afford things that are considered by the majority of the general public to be necessary items. Second, it calculates how many can be considered poor on the basis of being deprived of these items. The chapter's third section examines a wide range of social and economic characteristics of people who are classified as poor in these terms. The fourth section goes on to look at their attitudes and experiences – including the extent to which those defined by society as poor (or not) actually feel poor themselves. The final section looks separately and in more detail at this 'subjective' poverty, by measuring people's incomes against what they think is necessary to escape poverty according to three alternative definitions.

What items constitute the necessities of modern life?

What does a representative sample of the population believe to be the basic necessities of modern life? And how many people say they are unable to afford them?

Table 1 (page 14) ranks the percentage of respondents identifying different adult items as 'necessary' in 1999. Over 90 per cent of the population in each case perceive 'beds and bedding for everyone', 'heating to warm living areas of the home', a 'damp-free home', 'visiting friends or family in hospital' and 'medicines prescribed by doctor' as items which adults should have in Britain. By contrast, less than 10 per cent of the population sees a dishwasher, a mobile phone, Internet access or satellite television as necessary. Because goods introduced into the market often start as luxuries and, in later years, become necessities, we were anxious to test opinion about certain items that today are still only accessed by a minority.

As in the previous Breadline Britain surveys, items attracting 50 per cent or more support from the population, a 'democratic' majority, were considered as socially perceived necessities for the purposes of further analysis. In 1999, 35 of the 54 items in the adult list (Table 1) satisfied this criterion. This is important evidence that can help resolve public debate about what are and what are not the necessities of modern life. It also opens the way to searching investigation of the circumstances of those who lack a number or many of these necessities and particularly of those who identify them as necessities but do not have them and/or say they cannot afford them.

> ### The method used to define the necessities of life and how many people lack them
>
> The first stage of the research was to ask members of the general public about what items and activities they consider to define the living standards that everyone in Britain ought to be able to reach. The Office for National Statistics Omnibus Survey, in June 1999, asked a representative sample of people aged 16 and over to classify various items and activities. They had to sort cards containing 39 items and 15 activities relating to households, and 23 items and seven activities relating to children, into one of two categories. They were asked:
>
> *"I would like you to indicate the living standards you feel all adults (and children) should have in*

Britain today. Box A is for items which you think are necessary, which all adults should be able to afford and which they should not have to do without. Box B is for items which may be desirable but are not necessary."

This approach extended the methodology of the 1983 and 1990 Breadline Britain studies by adding items to the list of indicators of necessities – prompted partly by intervening research into social conditions, consumer behaviour and household interaction. The additional questions are to do mainly with goods and activities that are particularly relevant to children (see the next chapter) but also with social activities (which were relatively few in number in the first two surveys).

Having established, from the Omnibus Survey, which items more than 50 per cent of the population considered necessary, the main PSE survey, carried out later in 1999, sought to establish which sections of the population have these necessities and which sections cannot afford them. Respondents were asked:

"Now I'd like to show you a list of items and activities that relate to our standard of living. Please tell me which item you have or do not have by placing the cards on: Pile A for the items you have; Pile B for items you don't have but don't want; and Pile C for items you do not have and can't afford."

Table 1: Perception of adult necessities and how many people lack them (all figures show % of adult population)

	Omnibus Survey: items considered		Main stage survey: items that respondents	
	Necessary (%)	Not necessary (%)	Don't have, don't want (%)	Don't have, can't afford (%)
Beds and bedding for everyone	95	4	0.2	1
Heating to warm living areas of the home	94	5	0.4	1
Damp-free home	93	6	3	6
Visiting friends or family in hospital	92	7	8	3
Two meals a day	91	9	3	1
Medicines prescribed by doctor	90	9	5	1
Refrigerator	89	11	1	0.1
Fresh fruit and vegetables daily	86	13	7	4
Warm, waterproof coat	85	14	2	4
Replace or repair broken electrical goods	85	14	6	12
Visits to friends or family	84	15	3	2
Celebrations on special occasions such as Christmas	83	16	2	2
Money to keep home in a decent state of decoration	82	17	2	14
Visits to school, e.g. sports day	81	17	33	2
Attending weddings, funerals	80	19	3	3
Meat, fish or vegetarian equivalent every other day	79	19	4	3
Insurance of contents of dwelling	79	20	5	8
Hobby or leisure activity	78	20	12	7
Washing machine	76	22	3	1
Collect children from school	75	23	36	2

Table 1 Continued

	Omnibus Survey: items considered		Main stage survey: items that respondents	
	Necessary	Not necessary	Don't have, don't want	Don't have, can't afford
	(%)	(%)	(%)	(%)
Telephone	71	28	1	1
Appropriate clothes for job interviews	69	28	13	4
Deep freezer/fridge freezer	68	30	3	2
Carpets in living rooms and bedrooms	67	31	2	3
Regular savings (of £10 per month) for rainy days or retirement	66	32	7	25
Two pairs of all-weather shoes	64	34	4	5
Friends or family round for a meal	64	34	10	6
A small amount of money to spend on self weekly not on family	59	39	3	13
Television	56	43	1	1
Roast joint/vegetarian equivalent once a week	56	41	11	3
Presents for friends/family once a year	56	42	1	3
Holiday away from home once a year not with relatives	55	43	14	18
Replace worn out furniture	54	43	6	12
Dictionary	53	44	6	5
An outfit for social occasions	51	46	4	4
New, not second-hand, clothes	48	49	4	5
Attending place of worship	42	55	65	1
Car	38	59	12	10
Coach/train fares to visit friends/family quarterly	38	58	49	16
An evening out once a fortnight	37	56	22	15
Dressing gown	34	63	12	6
Having a daily newspaper	30	66	37	4
A meal in a restaurant/pub monthly	26	71	20	18
Microwave oven	23	73	16	3
Tumble dryer	20	75	33	7
Going to the pub once a fortnight	20	76	42	10
Video cassette recorder	19	78	7	2
Holidays abroad once a year	19	77	25	27
CD player	12	84	19	7
Home computer	11	85	42	15
Dishwasher	7	88	57	11
Mobile phone	7	88	48	7
Access to the Internet	6	89	54	16
Satellite television	5	90	56	7

Note: Percentage of people answering 'Don't know' not shown in table.

It is clear from the results in Table 1 that the general public holds ideas about the necessities of life that are more wide-ranging, or multidimensional, than is ordinarily represented in expert or political assessments. People of all ages and walks of life do not restrict their interpretation of 'necessities' to the basic material needs of a subsistence diet, shelter, clothing and fuel. There are *social customs, obligations* and *activities* that substantial majorities of the population also identify as among the top necessities of life.

Among the *customs* are 'celebrations on special occasions such as Christmas' (83 per cent) and 'attending weddings and funerals' (80 per cent). There are 'presents for friends/family once a year' (56 per cent). There are regular events to do with food, like a 'roast joint or the vegetarian equivalent once a week' (56 per cent), which extend our ideas of dietary needs well beyond the provision of the minimal calories required for physiological efficiency. The views on clothing needs extend ideas about basic cover to include 'a warm, waterproof coat' (85 per cent) and 'two pairs of all-weather shoes' (64 per cent).

Among the *obligations* and *activities* described as necessary are not just those which seem on the face of it to satisfy individual physiological survival and individual occupation – like a 'hobby or leisure activity' (78 per cent). They also include joint activities with friends and within families such as 'visits to friends or family' (84 per cent), especially those in hospital (92 per cent). They involve reciprocation and care of, or service for, others. People recognise the need to have friends or family round for a meal (64 per cent), for example.

What is striking is the strength of public acknowledgement that such social activities take their place among the 'necessities' of life. Analysis of the survey results showed that slightly more people specified one or more social activities among the necessities of life (95 per cent) than those specifying one or more items to do with housing, food, clothing and consumer durables, for example.

The Breadline Britain surveys of 1983 and 1990, forerunners of the present survey, had already confirmed that perceptions of 'necessities' were more broadly based than the corresponding assessments made by many economists and by governments in their policies and legislation. However, the evidence they had unearthed was treated with scepticism in some quarters. Perhaps because indicators of social deprivation were relatively few, compared with those of material deprivation, the implications of the conclusions may not have been fully grasped.

Another related interpretation of these results is that the public's perception of necessities reflects the conditions and dependencies of contemporary life – whether these are created by what is available in the market or by developments in social structure and interaction. Necessities are perceived relative to contemporary conditions. The evidence for this conclusion comes primarily from the comparative analysis of the successive surveys of 1983, 1990 and 1999 (see Chapter 4).

The 'consensual' approach to poverty assumes that there are few differences across different sections of the population over what they perceive as the necessities of life. We examined the extent to which this assumption held true in 1999 by examining how judgements varied amongst different groups. Although some important differences were highlighted, there was a remarkable homogeneity of views found between people of different age and gender, and among different socio-economic groups. Despite the differences, we can still talk of a social 'consensus' about necessary items for three reasons:

- the differences were relatively small - there was greater consensus about national living standards than there was common experience of those standards;

- much of the difference between groups was due to a smaller percentage of one group rating each item as necessary, rather than ranking the items in a different order;

- in very few cases did these differences affect whether or not 50 per cent of the groups classified an item as 'necessary'.

Differences in views of what constitute the necessities of life

The main conclusion from the survey was a remarkable similarity of views between different groups. However, some differences are worth noting.

Poorer groups were sometimes more likely than the better-off groups to consider certain items to be necessities: there was a marked difference, for example, in the case of carpets in living rooms and bedrooms and a television. Such differences seem to be partly explained by circumstances – more of the rich than of the poor live in centrally heated rooms, and fewer may consider carpets to be a necessity, for example.

Men were generally more likely than women to specify some items and activities as essential, particularly those relating to personal consumption. Examples were 'having a small amount of money to spend each week on yourself, not on your family', 'new, not second-hand clothes' and 'going to the pub once a fortnight'. This confirms previous research showing that women and men can have different priorities (Nyman, 1996; Payne and Pantazis, 1997; Goode et al., 1998).

Unsurprisingly, people aged over 30 considered, on average, more goods and activities as necessary than younger people (16 to 30 years). They were significantly more likely, for example, to consider a 'roast joint or its vegetarian equivalent' and a dressing gown as essential. Whilst there may exist important factors that account for individual differences, strong cultural shifts from one generation to the next may explain why younger people were generally inclined to choose fewer items as necessities of life. Chapter 4 examines in greater detail the finding that younger people seem to be making a more restricted choice of necessities than in the past.

For those items that the majority of the population thought were necessities, the PSE survey identified how many people have them and how many cannot afford them. The results are summarised in the third and fourth columns of Table 1. It is to be expected that those items the population are less likely to nominate as necessities are those that respondents to the PSE survey were most likely to say that they 'don't have, don't want' and 'don't have, can't afford'. However, four items were each owned by at least 80 per cent of respondents even though they were not considered necessities by the majority: 'new, not second-hand clothes', a video cassette recorder, a dressing gown and a microwave oven. Clearly, even though these are not considered necessary, most people want and possess them.

Conversely, there were some items which at least three-quarters of people consider necessary, but significant numbers are unable to afford: 6 per cent cannot afford a damp-free home, 12 per cent cannot afford to replace or repair broken electrical goods, 14 per cent do not have money to keep their home in a decent state of decoration, and 8 per cent cannot afford home contents insurance. However, of all the items considered a necessity by the majority of the population, the greatest number of people, 25 per cent, cannot afford regular savings (of £10 per month) for a rainy day or retirement, followed by 18 per cent who cannot afford a holiday away from home.

How many people are poor?

From the list of items in Table 1, we selected the 35 items considered by 50 per cent or more of respondents to be necessary for an acceptable standard of living in Britain at the end of the twentieth century. For each respondent, we then calculated the number of items that they did not have and could not afford. It can be seen, in Table 2, that 58 per cent were lacking no items because they could not afford them. A further 14 per cent were lacking only one of the items. The greatest number of items lacking was 21, by one respondent.

The approach used to determine how many people are poor

A statistical analysis indicated that six of the items did not add to the reliability or validity of the definition of deprivation of necessities in terms of distinguishing between rich and poor. These items – a television, a fridge, beds and bedding for everyone, a washing machine, medicines prescribed by a doctor, and a deep freezer/fridge freezer – were therefore dropped from the analysis. The statistical approach outlined in the introduction to establish an optimal poverty threshold then showed that an enforced lack of two necessities and a low income best discriminated between being 'poor' and 'not poor' (see Appendix 2 for details).

On this basis, people could be considered to be 'poor' if there were at least two socially defined necessities that they were unable to afford; otherwise they could be classified as 'not poor'. However, two further considerations are necessary, based on relationships between deprivation of necessities and incomes:

* Some people were unable to afford two necessities, but had relatively high incomes. These people could be classified as having *risen out of poverty* recently – for example, they had got a job but had not yet been able to buy all the basics.

* Some people did not lack two or more necessities, but had relatively low incomes. These could be classified as being *vulnerable to poverty* – for example, they may have recently seen their incomes fall through losing a job, but have not yet lost some of the items perceived to be necessities of life.

Therefore four groups can actually be defined – 'poor', 'those vulnerable to poverty', 'those who have recently risen out of poverty' and 'those who are not poor'.

Table 2: Number of items respondents 'don't have, can't afford'

Items lacking	Number	(%)	Cumulative %
0	891	58.1	58.1
1	218	14.2	72.3
2	87	5.7	78.0
3	73	4.8	82.8
4	50	3.2	86.0
5	34	2.2	88.3
6	32	2.1	90.4
7	22	1.4	91.8
8	19	1.3	93.0
9	22	1.4	94.5
10	18	1.2	95.7
11	13	0.8	96.5
12	11	0.7	97.2
13	17	1.1	98.3
14	10	0.6	99.0
15	7	0.5	99.4
16	2	0.1	99.6
17	2	0.2	99.7
18	2	0.1	99.8
19	1	0.1	99.9
21	1	0.0	100.0
Total	**1534**	**100.0**	**100.0**

Table 3: PSE survey poverty classifications

	Number	%
Poor	393	25.6
Vulnerable to poverty	158	10.3
Risen out of poverty	28	1.8
Not poor	955	62.2
Total	**1534**	**100.0**

On the basis of possession of necessities only, Table 2 shows that just over 72 per cent of people would be classified as not poor and just under 28 per cent as poor, with a poverty threshold set at being unable to afford two or more necessities (see box on page 18). However, 10 per cent had low enough incomes to make them vulnerable to poverty. Included in the 28 per cent who would have been classified as poor, on the basis of lacking two or more necessities, are around 2 per cent who had high enough incomes to suggest they had risen out of poverty, so that deprivation of these necessities did not seem likely to persist. This produces the four categories shown in Table 3.

The rest of this chapter concentrates on the 26 per cent whom this analysis has identified as poor.

Table 4: Who are the poor?

	Poverty rate (% in poverty)	Poverty proportion (% of all in poverty)	Number	Significance (see key p22)
All	25.6	100	1534	
Gender of respondent				**
Male	22	42	740	
Female	29	58	794	
Number of adults in the household				***
1	38	32	332	
2	22	50	919	
3+	25	18	282	
Number of children in the household				***
0	22	56	994	
1	29	16	210	
2	29	16	217	
3+	46	13	113	
Age of the youngest child				***
0-4	41	48	206	
5-11	35	35	175	
12-15	20	11	94	
16+	18	7	67	
Age of respondent				***
16-24	34	11	126	
25-34	38	27	284	
35-44	20	14	262	
45-54	25	16	253	
55-64	20	14	262	
65-74	21	10	195	
75+	21	8	154	

Table 4 Continued

	Poverty rate (% in poverty)	Poverty proportion (% of all in poverty)	Number	Significance (see key p22)
Age respondent completed education				***
<16	30	30	344	
16	33	31	311	
17	27	9	120	
18	24	8	111	
19+	17	22	426	
Region				**
North East	20	5	92	
North West	19	5	105	
Merseyside	29	3	41	
Yorks and Humberside	27	9	124	
East Midlands	23	7	124	
West Midlands	38	15	154	
Eastern	18	6	132	
London	30	12	155	
South East	22	11	205	
South West	24	9	147	
Wales	35	10	116	
Scotland	22	8	137	
Longstanding illness/disability in the household				**
No	23	57	963	
Yes	30	44	571	
Ethnicity				***
White	24	89	1466	
Black	(71)	(3)	(17)	
Indian	(37)	(2)	(19)	
Bangladeshi	(92)	(3)	(13)	
Other	(50)	(3)	(20)	
Employment status of household				***
1 worker	28	26	361	
2 workers	14	19	520	
3 workers	23	8	141	
No workers – retired	23	21	354	
No workers - sick/disabled	61	10	62	
No workers – unemployed	77	10	48	
No workers – other	76	8	38	

Table 4 Continued

	Poverty rate (% in poverty)	Poverty proportion (% of all in poverty)	Number	Significance (see key p22)
Marital status of respondent				***
Single	31	19	236	
Married	20	45	894	
Cohabiting	31	11	139	
Separated/divorced	46	16	135	
Widowed	30	10	131	
Household composition				***
Single adult	32	22	274	
Lone parent +1 child	66	5	29	
Lone parent +2 children	62	3	21	
Lone parent +3+ children	(89)	(2)	(9)	
Couple	15	18	485	
Couple +1 child	24	7	108	
Couple +2 children	26	11	172	
Couple +3 children	39	6	57	
Couple +4+ children	29	2	21	
2 or more adults no children	34	6	71	
2 or more adults with children	52	4	33	
Couple with one or more adults no children	21	9	159	
Couple with one or more adults and 1 child	13	2	56	
Couple with one or more adults and 2+ children	37	4	41	
Tenure				***
Outright owner	15	17	464	
Owner with mortgage	19	35	704	
Private tenant/other	33	9	110	
Housing association tenant	57	10	71	
Local authority tenant	61	29	185	
Receiving Income Support and Jobseeker's Allowance				***
No	21	73	1382	
Yes	70	27	152	
Household income				***
Below 60% PSE equivalent income	53	57	373	
Below 50% PSE equivalent income	53	44	279	
Below 40% PSE equivalent income	59	31	180	

Table 4 Continued

	Poverty rate (% in poverty)	Poverty proportion (% of all in poverty)	Number	Significance (see key below)
Quintile of PSE equivalent income				***
5 (highest)	0.6	0.6	197	
4	17	15	266	
3	24	19	266	
2	40	31	301	
1 (lowest)	59	34	309	
How far do you think you are above or below the level of income that is necessary to keep a household such as the one you live in out of poverty?				***
A lot above that level	5	6	470	
A little above that level	17	17	412	
About the same	38	19	189	
A little below that level	52	17	126	
A lot below that level	85	29	134	
Don't know	24	12	196	
*How far above or below the level of **absolute** poverty would you say your household is?*				***
A lot above that level	8	15	702	
A little above that level	25	20	307	
About the same	43	12	108	
A little below that level	74	19	102	
A lot below that level	79	23	115	
Don't know	22	11	192	
*How far above or below the level of **overall** poverty would you say your household is?*				***
A lot above that level	4	5	525	
A little above that level	16	14	339	
About the same	27	7	107	
A little below that level	54	19	138	
A lot below that level	80	40	196	
Don't know	25	14	221	

Key to significance levels: * < 0.05; **< 0.01; ***< 0.001

Note: Figures in brackets are based on twenty cases or fewer and are not reliable. All data in table are weighted

Who is poor?

Table 4 shows how the poverty rate (the percentage who are poor) varies according to the characteristics of the individual and the household they are living in. Thus, for example, in the second column, 22 per cent of male respondents were poor compared with 29 per cent of female respondents - confirming that poverty is more common for women. The third column shows the poverty proportion - what proportion of all the poor is made up of individuals/households with a given characteristic. So, for example, married people make up 45 per cent of all the poor, although the chances of a married person being poor is lower than average, at 20 per cent. The fourth column gives the number of people in the survey who were in the group; where this was below 20, the figures are in brackets to emphasise that the sample is too small to make reliable predictions for the whole population. For example, the poverty rates for the non-white ethnic groups are not reliable. The final column gives the level of the significance of the difference between the poverty rates observed.

For all respondents the average proportion of people who are poor is 25.6 per cent. There are some groups where the proportion is more than double this average rate:

- non-retired *people who are not working* because they are unemployed (77 per cent) or sick/disabled (61 per cent);
- *those on income support* (70 per cent);
- *lone parents* (62 per cent);
- *Local authority tenants* (61 per cent) and *housing association* tenants (57 per cent).

Although the number of respondents in the non-white ethnic groups is very small, the results indicate a much higher poverty rate for non-white ethnic groups especially among the Bangladeshi and Black ethnic groups.

Divorced or separated people are more likely to be poor (46 per cent) and there are also higher proportions of poor people in households of certain types:

- those with *3+ children* (46 per cent);
- those with *youngest child aged 0-4* (41 per cent) or aged 5-11 (35 per cent);
- households *with one adult* (38 per cent).

Younger people are also more likely to be poor:

- *16- to 24-year-olds* (34 per cent);
- *25- to 34-year-olds* (38 per cent).

Slightly greater proportions of *those finishing education below age 16* are poor (30 per cent) and those staying on to age 19 or above are much less likely to be poor (17 per cent).

In many ways, the data confirm other research in identifying the poorer groups. The survey also contained some questions on health perceptions that confirm an association between poverty and poor health. General Health Questionnaire (GHQ 12) scores are a measure of subjective well-being - the higher the score, the *worse* the well-being. Poor people scored 25.7 on average, compared with 22.0 on average for non-poor people. This difference is statistically significant at the 99.9 per cent level.

Of course, these socio-economic and demographic characteristics are not independent of each other: for example, being in receipt of Income Support is associated with being a lone parent or unemployed. The odds of living in poverty, *independent* of the other variables, can be calculated using multivariate analysis. This requires some of the categories to be somewhat differently defined to ensure sample sizes large enough to make the analysis valid. The results of this analysis are listed in Table 5.

The results show the effect of certain factors on the odds of being poor. In the first column ('bivariate' results), these relative odds are compared without taking account of any of the other variables. Relative odds in this case compare the chance of being poor with the odds of not being poor. So, for example, men have a 22 per cent chance of being poor and a 78 per cent of not, or relative odds of about 1:3.5. For women it is 29 per cent to 71 per cent, or 1:2.4. So women's relative odds of being poor are just over 40 per cent worse than those for men.

The problems of measuring low income

There are some interesting results in terms of the relationship of income to poverty that show what reservations have to be made about the comprehensiveness of narrow income measures on their own for identifying poor people and housholds. As would be expected, those in the lower two-fifths of the income distribution have a greater probability of being poor (59 per cent for the lowest fifth and 40 per cent for the second lowest). However, this means that over 40 per cent of the poorest fifth are *not* poor in terms of not suffering from multiple deprivation and that nearly a quarter of those in the middle fifth of the income distribution are poor in these terms. This finding highlights the difficulties that can arise when trying to measure poverty using just a single measure of income, taken at one point in time. A household's income levels may change rapidly from one week to the next but it is a household's command of financial resources over time that will determine if it becomes 'poor' or not.

There was a closer relationship between subjective assessments of the adequacy of income in relation to definitions of poverty lines and actually being poor. Eighty-five per cent of those who felt their income was a lot below what was necessary to keep households like theirs out of poverty were actually poor in terms of having both a low income and suffering from multiple deprivation of necessities. Eighty per cent of those who felt their income level was a lot below what would be necessary to keep households like theirs above the UN's definition of overall poverty were actually poor. Nearly four-fifths of those who thought their income level was a lot or a little below what would be necessary to pass above the UN's narrower definition of absolute poverty were also poor in these terms. This suggests that simple measurements of subjective poverty may be valuable in helping to understand the prevalence of poverty.

This partially reflects the fact that on average the income of those who are poor is below that of those who are not poor. Using a variety of scales for equivalent income the data show that the average income of the poor who lack necessities is about half that of people who are not poor in this sense:

	Poor	Not poor
Equivalent weekly income (PSE scale)	£183	£382
Equivalent weekly income (HBAI scale)	£205	£409
Equivalent weekly income (modified OECD scale)	£133	£267

(These differences are all statistically significant at the 0.001 per cent level.)

These differences are not large enough to be statistically significant in all cases – i.e. to be able to predict from the sample that there will be such a difference in the whole population. Where there is a significant difference, asterisks show the level of significance. For example, households with 'no worker – unemployed, sick or other' are more than 12 times more likely to be poor than households with two workers.

The second and third columns in Table 5 show the 'multivariate' results – the relative odds independent of the differences produced by interaction with other variables using two different models. The multivariate analysis requires there to be one measure of income only. There are two proxy measures for income in the analysis – income quintile and Income Support. The model in the second column therefore controls for all variables except Income Support and that in the third column controls for all variables except for income quintile and age completed education. In the former, the number of children, number of adults, marital status, household structure, region, age leaving full-time education and ethnicity no longer make a significant difference to the number in poverty. In the latter, some of these – marital status, household structure, region and ethnicity – once again have an impact.

These results suggest that many of the demographic characteristics that appear to be associated with poverty in Table 4 have this association mainly because they are associated with relatively low income. They therefore cease to have a significant

Table 5: The relative odds of being poor

	Bivariate: not taking account of other variables	Multivariate: controlling for other variables (except whether on Income Support)	Multivariate: controlling for other variables (except income quintile and education)
Gender of respondent			
Male	1.00	1.00	1.00
Female	1.42**	1.38*	1.37*
Number of children in the household			
0	1.00		
1	1.45*		
2	1.43*		
3+	3.02***		
Number of adults in the household			
1	2.23***		
2	1.00		
3+	1.17		
Age of respondent			
16-24	2.04**	4.81***	4.00**
25-34	2.44***	8.91***	4.57***
35-44	1.00	2.64*	1.51
45-54	1.35	6.26***	2.47**
55-64	1.02	3.31**	1.81
65-74	1.08	2.42**	1.54
75+	1.00	1.00	1.00
Employment status of household			
1 worker	2.05***	1.84**	2.27***
2+ workers	1.00	1.00	1.00
No workers - retired	1.58**	1.57	3.81**
No workers - unemployed, sick or other	12.92***	3.68***	6.49***
Marital status of respondent			
Single	1.90***		1.00
Married	1.00		2.73**
Cohabiting	1.85**		3.07**
Separated/divorced	3.52***		1.84
Widowed	1.73**		1.26
Household composition			
Single	2.67***		3.17**
Couple	1.00		1.00
Couple with children	2.16***		2.55***
Lone parent with children	11.66***		5.55***
Other	2.13***		2.88***

Table 5 Continued

	Bivariate: not taking account of other variables	Multivariate: controlling for other variables (except whether on Income Support)	Multivariate: controlling for other variables (except income quintile and education)
Region			
North	1.14		1.25
Midlands	1.71**		2.32**
South	1.00		1.44
London	1.62*		1.53
Wales	1.95**		2.36*
Scotland	1.06		1.00
Age respondent completed education			Not in this model
≤16	2.18***		
17/18	1.64*		
19+	1.00		
Ethnicity			
White	1.00		1.00
Not white	5.14***		4.90***
Tenure			
Owners	1.00	1.00	1.00
LA/HA tenants	7.15***	2.57***	4.06***
Private tenants other	2.30***	1.37	1.44
Receiving Income Support		Not in this model	
No	1.00		1.00
Yes	8.85***		2.48**
Income quintile			Not in this model
1 (lowest)	222.60***	159.87***	
2	100.84***	100.25***	
3	49.16***	51.35***	
4	31.63***	32.79***	
5 (highest)	1.00	1.00	

Note: Asterisks show the level of statistical significance

effect after controlling for income. This is not surprising. Those factors that in themselves are associated with deprivation of necessities of life even when the effect of income is taken out include being in a household with fewer workers, a lone parent, a member of a minority ethnic group, or living in social rented housing – and to a lesser extent being young and being female. These tend to confirm other studies of poverty. What is more notable is that even when controlling for all other factors, those on Income Support are much more likely to be in

poverty – suggesting that raising Income Support levels may be a well-targeted way of relieving poverty.

What do people in poverty experience?

So far, the analysis has been concerned with the characteristics of the poor - the association between poverty and the social and economic characteristics of poor people. However, one of the main objectives of the PSE survey is to explore the association

Table 6: Experiences and attitudes of people in poverty

Table 6a: Subjective personal experience and expectations of poverty

	Proportion of those answering this way who are poor	Proportion of poor people who answer this way	Number of people answering this way	Significance (see key p29)
Do you think that you can genuinely say you are poor				
All the time?	86	23	102	***
Sometimes?	58	45	302	
Never?	11	32	1120	
Looking back over your life, how often have there been times in your life				
when you think you have lived in poverty by the standards of that time?				
Never	14	33	906	***
Rarely	30	15	200	
Occasionally	44	33	291	
Often	56	15	105	
Most of the time	59	4	29	
Has anything happened recently (in the last two years) in your life which has				
Improved your standard of living?	17	12	272	
Reduced your standard of living?	54	21	152	
Increased your income?	19	17	366	
Reduced your income?	41	24	235	
None of these?	24	48	791	
Is there anything that you expect to happen in the near future (in the next two years) in your life which will				
Improve your standard of living?	32	19	232	
Reduce your standard of living?	39	10	95	
Increase your income?	28	24	338	
Reduce your income?	26	9	128	
None of these?	23	55	920	

Note: Proportions add to more than 100 because multiple responses possible

Table 6 continues overleaf

between poverty and other experiences, including social exclusion. Social exclusion is analysed more fully in Chapter 5. In this section, selected data collected in the PSE survey are used to explore the relationship between being poor and other experiences. They are summarised in Table 6.

The first two questions are concerned with perceptions of the experience of poverty now and in the past. (Subjective perceptions of poverty using several definitions are also explored further in the next section: these questions simply asked people about whether they felt poor without defining what poor means.) It is not surprising that most of those who say that they are 'poor all the time' (86 per cent) were found in the survey to be poor. However, it is more surprising that, of those who say they are 'never poor', 11 per cent were found to be poor in terms of lacking necessities and they constitute nearly a third of poor people. These results indicate

Table 6b: Perception of poverty and its causes in Britain in general

	Proportion of those answering this way who are poor	Proportion of poor people who answer this way	Number of people answering this way	Significance (see key p29)
Over the last ten years, do you think poverty has been				
Increasing?	30	52	670	***
Decreasing?	16	13	301	
Staying about the same?	22	26	462	
Don't know	29	7	100	
Over the next ten years, do you think poverty will				
Increase?	30	46	610	***
Decrease?	18	16	353	
Stay at the same level?	24	28	435	
Don't know	29	7	100	
Why, in your opinion, are there people who live in need?				
Because they have been unlucky	24	12	192	NS
Because of laziness and lack of willpower	21	23	409	
Because there is much injustice in our society	28	35	476	
It's an inevitable part of modern progress	25	24	362	
None of these	27	6	78	

Table 6c: Security and satisfaction with area you live in

	Proportion of those answering this way who are poor	Proportion of poor people who answer this way	Number of people answering this way	Significance (see key p29)
How satisfied are you with this area as a place to live?				
Very satisfied	19	41	843	***
Fairly satisfied	29	35	472	
Neither satisfied nor dissatisfied	48	7	61	
Slightly dissatisfied	41	11	104	
Very dissatisfied	48	6	52	
How safe do you feel walking alone in this area after dark?				
Very safe	17	18	397	***
Fairly safe	26	45	676	
A bit unsafe	30	27	349	
Very unsafe	38	10	105	
How safe do you feel when you are alone in your home at night?				
Very safe	21	44	812	***
Fairly safe	27	39	561	
A bit unsafe	44	14	124	
Very unsafe	45	4	31	

Table 6d: Civic involvement

	Proportion of those answering this way who are poor	Proportion of poor people who answer this way	Number of people answering this way	Significance (see key below)
Participation in civic life				
Non-participative	43	20	180	***
Moderately participative	28	53	743	
Highly participative	18	27	610	

Table 6e: Impact of lack of money on well-being

	Proportion of those answering this way who are poor	Proportion of poor people who answer this way	Number of people answering this way	Significance (see key p29)
Have there been times in the past year when, as a result of a lack of money, you've felt isolated and cut off from society or depressed?				
Neither of these	15	43	1126	
Yes, isolated	74	23	120	
No, not isolated	26	5	75	
Yes, depressed	70	43	243	
No, not depressed	25	8	1119	

Key to significance levels:
* <0.05; **<0.01; ***<0.001

Note: Proportions add to more than 100 because multiple responses possible

that some people have relatively low expectations in that they do not consider themselves poor even though they lack necessities of life.

There is also a strong relationship between poverty in the present and people's experiences of lifetime poverty. The more often they believe that they have been poor in the past, the more likely they are to be found to be poor at present.

Half of people who had experienced a reduction in their standard of living in the last two years were now poor. Those who expected a change in their standard of living were more likely to be poor – whether the change was expected to be upwards or downwards.

The other questions reviewed in Table 6 show that:

- Poor people are more likely than others to blame injustice, and less likely to blame laziness and a lack of will-power, for the fact that people live in need. Nevertheless, most poor people do not blame injustice. Nearly a quarter do blame laziness and lack of will-power and a further quarter think it is an inevitable result of modern progress.

- People whose *satisfaction with their local environment is low* are more likely to be poor. Those who are dissatisfied with their area, or who feel unsafe walking about their neighbourhood or being alone in their homes, are more likely than average to live in poverty. Note, however, that this does not mean that most poor people are dissatisfied in these ways: although, for example, nearly half of the people

Table 7: Income needed each week to keep a household of *your* type out of absolute, overall and general poverty (Britain 1999)

	Absolute poverty	Overall poverty	General poverty
Mean income needed	£178	£239	£219
Don't know	18%	21%	17%
	(%)	(%)	(%)
Actual income a lot above	52	34	34
A little above	24	26	31
About the same	8	8	14
A little below	8	11	10
A lot below	9	15	10
Total (excluding don't knows)	**100**	**100**	**100**
Number	**1252**	**1213**	**1273**

very dissatisfied with their area are poor, this represents only 6 per cent of all poor people.

- Poor people are much less likely to be active in their local communities than people who are not poor. This finding is based on two questions - membership of organisations and participation in civic affairs - used to create a classification of civic participation.

- Nearly three-quarters of people who feel isolated and/or depressed as a result of lack of money during the last year are currently poor. Chapter 5 considers further the theme of isolation with respect to social exclusion.

Subjective assessments of poverty

Finally this chapter presents some results using three subjective measures of poverty.

As outlined in Chapter 1, the World Summit for Social Development in 1995 proposed a distinction between absolute and overall poverty. In the PSE survey, these ideas were adapted to conditions in Britain. In addition, respondents were asked to determine whether their income was 'below the level of income you think is necessary to keep a household such as yours out of poverty' – in the tables below we describe this as 'general' poverty.

It can be seen in Table 7 that as many as 17 per cent of the sample said they had less income than the level they identified as being enough to keep a household like theirs out of 'absolute' poverty. The income, after tax, said to be needed each week to escape 'absolute' poverty averaged £178 for all households. Some informants gave estimates widely different from this average but the great majority, allowing for type of household, were within 20 per cent of this figure.

Perceptions of the 'poverty line' varied by type of household, as would be expected. More lone parents than any other type of household (54 per cent with two children) said they had an income below that needed to keep out of absolute poverty (Table 8). Next were single pensioners (24 per cent) and single adults (20 per cent). The average for all households was 14 per cent.

A larger proportion (26 per cent) ranked themselves in 'overall' poverty (Table 7). Again, lone parents and single pensioners were more likely to claim that they had incomes below this level. It is interesting that the assessment of the mean income needed to keep a household out of 'general' poverty (see above) fell between the absolute and overall standard, which indicates that respondents are capable of making a distinction between these various subjective thresholds.

Table 8: Percentage of each type of household reporting their actual income as lower than the amount they needed to keep out of absolute, overall and general poverty (Britain 1999)

	Absolute poverty (%)	Overall poverty (%)	General poverty (%)
Single pensioner	24	37	27
Couple pensioner	18	26	22
Single adult	20	29	24
Couple	11	14	13
Couple 1 child	15	28	29
Couple 2 children	9	23	13
Couple 3+ children	10	25	25
Lone parent 1 child	41	56	54
Lone parent 2+ children	54	71	62
Other	19	27	14
All households	**17**	**26**	**20**

It is striking that 1 in 6 people in a rich industrial society perceive that their incomes are insufficient to meet the very basic needs defined by an absolute poverty threshold, and that over a quarter consider themselves in overall poverty. These levels are much higher than is generally assumed in national and international discourse.

3 Child poverty in Britain

Introduction

In March 1999, the Prime Minister declared that the Labour Government was on a "twenty-year mission" to "end child poverty forever" (Blair, 1999). This commitment was made against the backdrop of a threefold increase in child poverty (measured in terms of relative income) between 1979 and the 1990s (see Chapter 1). By 1998/9, over a third of British children were living in households with incomes below 50 per cent of the average – the measure of childhood poverty most commonly used (DSS, 2000).

There are a number of limitations on using household income to measure poverty among children. First, income measures assume that children share the living standards of their family – if the household as a whole is poor, then children in that household must also be poor. In other words, it is assumed that household income is distributed evenly among household members. Yet there is some evidence to suggest that spending on children is relatively similar in all families. This therefore means that in poorer families spending on children is, as a proportion of income, disproportionately higher than the average (Middleton et al., 1997). Other evidence demonstrates that women's share of family income is disproportionately small (Goode et al., 1998; Middleton et al., 1997). Second, household income measures of childhood poverty are difficult to explain in simple terms and tell us little or nothing about how poverty impacts on children's lives. Direct measures of children's individual living standards can identify not simply how many children are poor, but how poverty affects children. What should children in Britain have and experience if they are to avoid poverty, and what do poor children go without that non-poor children do not?

The approach to defining and measuring poverty used for the present survey, based on socially perceived necessities, is particularly well suited to measuring childhood poverty. It allows the definition of childhood poverty to be democratically decided and can produce a poverty line specifically related to children, rather than to adults or households. The meaning of poverty in children's lives can, therefore, be better understood. The approach used is described in the box below.

The method used to define the necessities of life and how many children lack them

A 'democratic poverty measure' specifically related to children was originally developed for the Small Fortunes Survey of the lifestyles and living standards of British children (Middleton et al., 1997). In this survey, a list of children's items and activities built upon the six items specifically relating to children in the original Breadline Britain studies, and was drawn up following extensive research with 200 mothers from a range of social groups and income levels about the basic needs of children in Britain (Middleton et al., 1994). The list was subjected to further scrutiny in another series of focus groups held as part of the development work for the Poverty and Social Exclusion Survey (Bradshaw et al., 1998). The final list included 30 items and activities for children.

This list was included as part of the Office for National Statistics' Omnibus Survey in June of 1999 (see Appendix 4) to establish what are socially perceived necessities for children. In this chapter, parents' judgements of what are necessities for children are used, rather than those of the adult population as a whole. The differences between the judgements of parents and all adults were very small (see Table 14, page 49). Furthermore, since the unit of analysis throughout this chapter is the child and

since it is parents who decide what children will have, it is more appropriate to use the judgements of parents. This is also consistent with the method used for the Small Fortunes study.

In the PSE survey, parents were asked to distinguish whether their children (considered together in each family rather than individually) had each item or activity, did not have it because the parent did not want it, or did not have it because they could not afford it. As in the analysis in Chapter 2, this chapter focuses on children's lack of items and/or activities that parents could not afford, rather than chose not to buy.

In addition to using the views of parents rather than all adults to determine what are considered necessities, there are two other major differences between the analysis of adult poverty and child poverty in this report. The first is that because the overall sample was smaller, it was not possible to do the statistical analysis that, in the adult work, led to the elimination of items that did not add to the definition of poverty, so all items that more than 50 per cent of parents defined as necessary are used throughout. The second is that it was considered inappropriate to remove children in households that were potentially rising out of poverty from the definition of poor because it was not known whether higher levels of income would be transferred into extra spending on children.

This chapter presents the results of the survey for children. As with the adult chapter, it begins by considering which of the various items and activities members of the public regard as necessities for children and then the proportion of children that live in households unable to afford items that the majority of people regard as necessary. The analysis goes on to define a poverty threshold, and then investigates the characteristics of children who fall below it. Next, the chapter identifies the independent effect of various characteristics to suggest some of the reasons behind childhood poverty. A final section draws some important conclusions for public policy.

What items are considered to necessities for children?

Of the 30 children's items and activities in the survey, all but three were thought to be necessities more than 50 per cent of parents. The exceptions, shown in italics in Table 9, were 'at least 50p a week for sweets', 'computer suitable for schoolwork', and 'computer games'.

Most of the remaining items were believed to be necessities by well over 50 per cent of parents; and over half (16 out of 30) of the items were believed to be necessities by at least 75 per cent. This contrasts with the adult measure, for which 35 out of 54 items crossed the 50 per cent threshold (65 per cent of items) and just 20 items were endorsed by 75 per cent or more of adults (37 per cent of items).

In general, those items that might be regarded as essential for the physical well-being of the child – food, clothing and household items such as beds and bedding – were believed to be necessities by larger percentages of parents than were items for the child's social or educational development. However, there are some interesting exceptions to this. Having 'meat, fish or a vegetarian equivalent at least twice a day' was thought to be necessary by fewer respondents than, for example, 'educational games', a 'hobby or leisure activity' and attending 'play group at least once a week for pre-school age children'.

Which necessities do children lack?

For each of these socially perceived necessities, only a small proportion of children have parents who cannot afford them (the relevant percentages are shown in the second column of Table 9). They are least likely to go without items that the largest percentages of parents thought to be necessary - food, environmental and developmental items - and most likely to lack participation items and activities.

Nearly all parents think that 'new, properly fitted, shoes', 'a warm waterproof coat' and 'fresh fruit or vegetables at least once a day' are necessities, yet 1 in 50 children do not have these because of lack of money. One in 25 go without each of the following

Table 9: Necessities and 'necessities deprivation'

	Percentage of parents regarding item as 'necessary'	Percentage of children who lack item because their parents cannot afford it		
		All children	Children who lack at least one of the 27 necessary items	Children who lack at least two of the 27 necessary items
Food				
Fresh fruit or vegetables at least once a day	93	1.8	5	9
Three meals a day	91	(0.9)	(3)	(5)
Meat, fish or vegetarian equivalent at least twice a day	76	3.7	11	21
Clothes				
New, properly fitted, shoes	96	2.3	7	12
Warm, waterproof coat	95	1.9	6	11
All required school uniform*	88	2.0	6	12
At least 7 pairs of new underpants	84	1.9	6	11
At least 4 pairs of trousers	74	3.1	9	18
At least 4 jumpers/cardigans/sweatshirts	71	2.8	8	16
Some new, not second-hand, clothes	67	3.1	9	18
Participation and activities				
Celebrations on special occasions	92	3.6	10	20
Hobby or leisure activity*	88	3.2	9	18
School trip at least once a term*	73	1.8	5	(10)
Swimming at least once a month	71	7.1	21	34
Holiday away from home at least one week a year	63	21.8	64	68
Leisure equipment*	57	3.1	9	17
Friends round for tea/snack fortnightly*	53	3.7	11	21
Developmental				
Books of own	90	(0.1)	0	(1)
Play group at least once a week (pre-school age children)*	89	(1.3)	(4)	(7)
Educational games	84	4.2	12	21
Toys (e.g. dolls, teddies)*	85	(0.5)	(1)	(3)
Construction toys	66	3.3	10	19
Bike: new/second-hand*	60	3.4	10	18
At least 50p a week for sweets	45	1.6	-	-
Computer suitable for schoolwork	38	35.7	-	-
Computer games	13	13.2	-	-
Environmental				
A bed and bedding for self	96	(0.6)	(2)	(3)
Bedroom for every child of different sex over 10 years*	76	3.3	10	10
Carpet in bedroom	75	(1.4)	(4)	(5)
Garden to play in	68	3.5	10	8
Base	560	792	273	139

Notes: *Figures in brackets indicate less than 20 unweighted cases*
Items in italics were thought to be necessities by less than 50% of parents
* *age-related items*

highly endorsed necessities: 'celebrations on special occasions such as birthdays', 'educational games', 'meat, fish or vegetarian equivalent at least twice a day', and a 'garden to play in'. The necessity that the largest proportion of children goes without is a 'holiday away from home once a year', lacked by over one-fifth of children. The second highest is 'swimming at least once a month', which more than 1 in 15 children go without.

How many children fall below the child poverty threshold?

A similar range of statistical techniques to those used for adults (Appendix 3) have been used to determine a threshold for childhood necessities deprivation. This statistical analysis suggests that a child should be considered to be deprived if lacking any one or more of the items in the list because their parents cannot afford them. A third of children – 34 per cent – are poor, or 'necessity-deprived', by this definition. However, since a large proportion of children lacked one item in particular (a 'holiday away from home once a year'), it seems sensible also to use a more restrictive deprivation threshold of two or more items. Eighteen per cent of children are poor by this definition.

The last two columns of Table 9 show that a child defined as poor has a much greater than average risk of being deprived of each of the items listed. If a child lacks at least one item, their chance of lacking any specific item is in most cases at least three times the average. If the deprivation threshold is set at two items rather than one, the chance of a deprived child lacking any specific necessity doubles once again in most cases.

Which children are poor?

Once necessities deprivation thresholds have been set, it is possible to explore whether particular groups of children are more likely to be deprived than others (Table 10). A range of family, economic and demographic characteristics significantly increase the risk of a child being necessities deprived.

Employment status

The employment status of the household has a large impact on levels of childhood necessities deprivation. The proportions of deprived children in households where there are no workers are double those for children as a whole. Nearly two-thirds of children in jobless households lack one or more item and two-fifths are deprived of at least two.

Children with two (or more) adults in the household in paid work are the least likely to be deprived. However, having working parents in paid employment does not necessarily protect children from deprivation, particularly when the paid work is part-time. Over half of children with one or more parents working part-time go without at least one item and three in ten lack two or more.

Child poverty and low household income

As was found in the adult analysis there is not a complete correlation between income and child poverty in terms of necessity deprivation (Figure 3). For a poverty threshold set at lacking one or more socially perceived necessity, almost one half of children (45 per cent) who live in households that are 'income poor'* are not 'necessities deprived'. At the higher threshold of going without two or more necessities, almost two-thirds of children (65 per cent) are income poor but not necessities deprived.

The explanation may lie in the evidence, referred to above, that poverty is not always shared evenly among household members. These data suggest that parents in many income poor households are able to protect their children from necessities deprivation, presumably by ensuring that children take priority in the allocation of available income. An alternative explanation might lie in the length of time for which households have been below the income poverty line. Households that have only recently fallen below the income poverty line and/or who have incomes close to it may be able to continue to protect their children from necessities deprivation for some time after this fall.

* defined as below 60 per cent of median equivalised household income

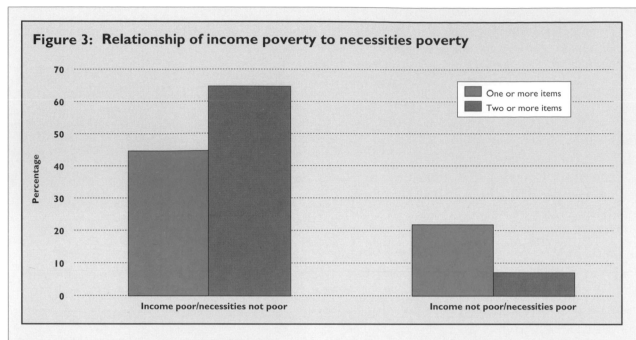

Figure 3: Relationship of income poverty to necessities poverty

This does not necessarily mean that children living above the income poverty threshold escape poverty in terms of being deprived of necessities. But as Figure 3 shows, most do. Only one-fifth of children who are not income poor are deprived of one or more items and only 7 per cent of two or more items (this compares with 34 per cent and 18 per cent respectively of all children – see below). There are at least two possible explanations for why this small group of children are not income poor but are necessities poor. First, these children may live in households whose incomes are very close to the poverty line and/or whose incomes might only recently have climbed above the line following a lengthy period of income poverty. Second, the income measure takes no account of housing costs. It may be that these children live in households with relatively high housing costs, leaving less for the purchase of children's necessities.

Household type

Households with children have been divided into lone parents (18 per cent of children), couples (69 per cent) and others (13 per cent). Children whose parents are a couple (and live without other adults in the household) are the least likely to be necessities deprived. Children in lone parent families are the most likely to be necessities deprived and are almost twice as likely as children in couple households to go without one item and three times more likely to be lacking two or more items.

Income

As would be expected, the lower the income quintile the child's household is in, the more likely the child is to be necessities deprived, because their parents cannot afford items.

Over two-thirds of children in the lowest income quintile are deprived using the one item threshold and more than one-third are deprived using the two or more item measure. However, deprivation is not confined to those in the lowest income quintiles. Thirteen per cent of children in the top two quintiles are deprived of at least one item. Possible reasons for this have already been described above.

Age of child

In general, deprivation of necessities decreases with the child's age. However, most of this variation is not significant. The exception is for children aged between two and four years, who are significantly more likely to lack two or more items than the other age groups. This may be because it is particularly costly to provide pre-school children with the items and activities in the list. For example, clothing will need replacing more regularly for this age group, as the rate of growth is at its most rapid.

Table 10: Characteristics of 'necessities deprived' children

	Percentage of children lacking one or more item	Percentage of children lacking two or more items
Employment status of household*		
2 full-time/more than 2 workers	32	(15)
1 full-time, 1 part-time	19	(6)
1 full-time	37	19
1 or more part-time	52	30
No workers	63	42
Household type*		
Couple	29	11
Lone parent	52	33
Other	39	13
Income quintile*		
4 and 5 (highest)	(13)	(4)
3	28	(7)
2	27	14
1 (lowest)	67	37
Age of child		
0 to 1	36	(16)
2 to 4‡	37	23
5 to 10	37	17
11 to 16	29	15
Number of children in household*		
1	29	13
2	25	11
3	42	25
4+	68	39
Child has long-standing illness		
No	36	19
Yes	34	13
Respondent has long-standing illness*		
No	32	16
Yes	41	24
Ethnicity*		
White	30	14
Non-white	54	35
Tenure*		
Own	24	11
Local authority rented	69	41
Other rented	57	34

Table 10 Continued

	Percentage of children lacking one or more item	Percentage of children lacking two or more items
*Member of household in receipt of IS or JSA**		
No	28	12
Yes	66	43
Total	34	18

Note: Figures in brackets indicate less than 20 unweighted cases
     * significant differences between all groups on both deprivation measures (p < 0.05)
     ‡ significant difference between this age group and others on two or more item deprivation (p < 0.05)
     IS - Income Support; JSA - Jobseeker's Allowance

Number of children

There is no significant difference between the proportion of children with no siblings and with one sibling being deprived using either the one or two item threshold. However, the deprivation levels of children in households with three or more children increase dramatically.

Illness and disability

The differences between the deprivation of children with and without a long-standing illness are not significant. This suggests that, despite the extra cost of bringing up a child with a disability and the pressures this places on parents' ability to work, they are still largely protected from going without (Dobson and Middleton, 1998).

However, parents who themselves have a long-standing illness find it more difficult to protect their children from deprivation. Children who have at least one parent or household member with a long-standing illness are approximately a third more likely to be deprived than children as a whole, using either measure.

Ethnicity

Although there was widespread agreement between white and non-white parents as to what are necessities for children, the parents of non-white children are more likely to be unable to afford them.

Over one-half of non-white children are deprived of at least one item and over one-third of at least two.

Further analysis confirms the findings of other studies and suggests a number of possible reasons for this (HM Treasury, 1999). First, non-white children are more likely to be in larger families, in terms of the numbers of adults and children. Second, they are more likely to be in households with incomes in the lowest quintile. Finally, non-white children are more likely to live in jobless households. All of these characteristics have been shown above to be associated with high levels of deprivation.

Tenure

Children living in owner-occupied housing (that is, owned outright or with a mortgage) are far less likely to be necessities deprived than children in the rented sector. Children in local authority housing are the most likely to be deprived, with over two-thirds of this group lacking one or more item and two in five going without two or more. Again, there are connections with other findings. Children in local authority accommodation are more likely than average to be in lone parent families, non-working families, and in the lowest income quintile (ibid.).

Benefit receipt

Children in households that receive Income Support and/or Jobseeker's Allowance are far more likely to be necessities deprived than those children whose household members do not. They are nearly $2^1/_2$ times more likely to be deprived of one necessity and over $3^1/_2$ times more likely to be deprived of two or more.

Why are children poor?

The analysis so far has shown that certain subgroups of children with particular family, economic and demographic characteristics are significantly more likely to be necessities deprived than others. These characteristics need to be disentangled in order to separate out those that are most likely to place children at an increased risk of necessities deprivation when all other characteristics are taken into account.

A similar statistical analysis was carried out as for adults, to establish the independent effect of each factor found to increase the risk of deprivation.[1] Table 11 shows for each factor the relative odds of being deprived, in each instance setting a 'base case' of 1.00.

Necessities deprived – one item threshold
For children deprived of one or more items, employment status is not significantly associated with an increased risk of necessity deprivation when all other characteristics (including income) are taken into account. However, other characteristics are significant:

* children in households with additional adults (i.e. other than parents) are half as likely to be deprived as those in couple households;

* children in households in the lowest income quintile are over 4$\frac{1}{2}$ times as likely to be deprived than those in the two highest quintiles;

* the number of children in the family is significantly associated with deprivation. Every additional child in the family increases the risk that each child will be necessities deprived by 1$\frac{1}{2}$ times;

* children in local authority housing are over 4 times, and those in the 'other' rented sector over 2$\frac{1}{2}$ times, as likely to be deprived than children in owner-occupied households;

* children in households where the respondent to the survey has a long-standing illness are over 1$\frac{1}{2}$ times as likely to be deprived;

* children in households where one or more adults receive Income Support or Jobseeker's Allowance are over 3 times as likely to be deprived;

* children in lone parent households are not significantly more likely to be deprived than those in a couple household when other characteristics are taken into account. Therefore, although a child in a lone parent family has a significantly higher risk of being deprived of necessities (as shown above), this is nothing to do with lone parenthood in itself. Rather it is because lone parents are more likely to be living in local authority rented housing and in receipt of Income Support.

Necessities deprived – two items or more
For children deprived of two or more items, by contrast, employment status of the household is highly significant in predicting deprivation. Compared with children in households where two adults are in full-time work, or more than two adults are in employment, children:

* in households with one full-time and one part-time paid worker are 5 times as likely to be deprived;

* in households with one full-time paid worker are 8 times as likely to be deprived;

* in households with one or more part-time paid workers are 11 times as likely to be deprived;

* in households with no paid workers are 9 times as likely to be deprived.

The only other significant characteristic in this model is tenure. Children in local authority housing are three times and those in the 'other' rented sector over twice, as likely to be deprived than children in owner-occupied households.

The very different results produced by the two thresholds reflect differences between the household employment profiles of those children who are deprived of none, one, and two or more necessities.

Table 11: Logistic regression model predicting necessities deprivation

	Odds of child lacking one or more item	Odds of child lacking two or more items
Employment status of household		
2 full-time/more than 2 workers	1.00	1.00
1 full-time, 1 part-time	0.72	5.19*
1 full-time	1.11	8.32*
1 or more part-time	1.24	11.09**
No workers	0.60	8.87*
Household type		
Couple	1.00	1.00
Lone parent	0.54	0.82
Other	0.45*	0.89
Income quintile		
4 and 5 (highest)	1.00	1.00
3	2.58**	1.22
2	1.37	1.40
1 (lowest)	4.65***	2.31
Number of children in household		
One	1.00	1.00
For every increase in child	1.55***	1.14
Ethnicity		
White	1.00	1.00
Non-white	1.62	1.49
Tenure		
Own	1.00	1.00
LA rent	4.15***	2.94**
Other rent	2.64***	2.10*
Respondent had long-standing illness		
No	1.00	1.00
Yes	1.58*	1.55
Member of household in receipt of IS or JSA		
No	1.00	1.00
Yes	3.10*	2.15

Note: Significance * < 0.05; ** < 0.01; *** < 0.001

IS – Income Support; JSA – Jobseeker's Allowance

Almost half of children who lack one or more item are, in fact, deprived of only one necessity. These children are approximately evenly distributed among the various household employment statuses. In other words, going without just one item varies very little according to employment status of parents. Once the deprivation threshold is raised to two or more items, almost all of the children in two-worker households are removed from deprivation, because they lack only one item. Far higher proportions of children from part-time working households and those in jobless households remain in deprivation (as they lack two or more items). This seems to suggest that the two-item threshold is probably more valuable as a deprivation measure (see above).

The finding that children in a jobless household are less likely to be in deprivation than children in households with one or more part-time worker is probably the result of other variables impacting upon this, in particular benefit receipt and tenure.

As with one-item deprivation, for children in lone parent families it is not their family status per se that explains their deprivation, but rather the greater likelihood that they are in households with one or no paid workers or living in local authority rented housing.

Policy implications

This analysis has a number of important implications for policy. According to the Government, joblessness is a major cause of childhood poverty (HM Treasury, 2000, p7). A large part of their proposed solution for childhood poverty is to get parents into work. These findings have shown that employment is indeed vital to ensuring that children are not deprived of necessities, using a threshold of 'going without two or more necessities'. Children in jobless households are nine times more likely to be deprived than those with two or more paid workers in the household.

However, the Government has also recognised that "changes in the labour market have also increased the risk of poverty for children whose parents are in work" (ibid., p8). Their parallel commitment to 'make work pay' appears equally important to that of

reducing the number of jobless households, as children in households with only one worker, full- or part-time, are also much more likely to be necessities deprived than children in households with two full-time workers. Work per se will not keep children out of poverty and, for those households where the opportunity for two full-time salaries is simply not available and/or for those households where one parent wishes to stay at home to care for children, other policy avenues need to be explored.

Our evidence points to anomalies in some government policies if childhood poverty is to be eradicated. Many benefits for children give disproportionate emphasis to the needs of smaller families. Child Benefit is paid at a higher rate for the only or oldest child than for subsequent children and the Government continues to increase this gap. The Childcare Tax Credit provides for up to double the level of support for one child (£100) than for a second and, indeed, all subsequent children (a maximum of £150 is allowed for two or more children). The Family Premium on Income Support is paid at a flat rate to families with children, irrespective of how many children are in the family. All of these benefits will therefore favour disproportionately families with fewer children. Yet the risk of poverty clearly increases as the number of children in the family increases.

Tenure is also significantly related to poverty. Children in local authority housing are three times more likely to be deprived (using the two or more item threshold) than those in owner-occupied homes. For those in the private rented sector, the odds of being deprived are twice as high. This is even though employment status and income (amongst other characteristics) have been controlled for. It is to be hoped that the Government's National Strategy for Neighbourhood Renewal, the New Deal for Communities, and other initiatives to improve deprived neighbourhoods, will help to tackle the particular problem of poverty among children in local authority housing.

Defining and measuring childhood poverty as 'going without necessities that the majority of parents believe to be necessary, because parents cannot afford to provide them' has a number of advantages. First, and most important, it is a direct measure of poverty among children. This contrasts with indirect measures such as household income, which can tell us only whether the family is poor but reveal nothing about children's own direct experience of poverty. Second, it has shown that small but significant percentages of children go without food and clothing items that almost all parents believe to be necessary and which are widely accepted as being vital to the continued health and development of children. Finally, it allows other indicators to be identified which the Government might wish to focus on in its programme to reduce, and eventually abolish, childhood poverty.

Note

1   A logistic regression analysis was undertaken in which all of
    the characteristics that were found to be significantly
    associated with an increased risk of deprivation in the previous
    analysis were included in the model.

4 The growth of poverty in Britain

. . . .

The Poverty and Social Exclusion Survey was the third in the past two decades to measure how many people in Britain are unable to afford socially perceived necessities. By repeating a similar exercise in 1983, 1990 and 1999, we can get a picture of how poverty has changed over time. Although the surveys have not been identical, they have enough common data to allow several types of change to be charted:

- changes in the items that the majority of the population consider to be necessities of modern life;

- changes in how many people are deprived of each necessity, because they cannot afford it;

- changes in poverty defined as not having and being unable to afford a range of the necessities of life;

- changes in the number of people suffering from long-term poverty.

Changes in perception of necessities

Chapters 2 and 3 set out how the 1999 Omnibus Survey produced a consensual measure of deprivation by looking at which items were considered as necessities by the majority of the population. In 1983 and 1990, members of the general public were asked whether they considered specified items to be necessities. Since the first survey, in 1983, the responses have repeatedly confirmed the assumption on which this 'consensual' method has been based - that there is a high degree of consensus across different groups in the population about which items are necessities (Mack and Lansley, 1985).

Over time, if societies get richer, the relative theory of poverty predicts that the number of people who perceive common possessions and activities as necessary will increase. This is precisely what occurred between the 1983 and 1990 surveys: a higher percentage of respondents rated as necessities 30 out of 33 items common to both surveys.

On average, the British population has become richer throughout the 1980s and 1990s: between 1983 and 1998/9, average income rose by 51 per cent (after housing costs), from £9,932 per year (£191 per week) to £15,028 per year (£289 per week), at February 2000 prices.[1] This increase in incomes was not shared equally. The incomes and wealth of the 'richest' people increased considerably over the 1980s and 1990s while the incomes and wealth of the 'poorest' declined in real terms after allowing for inflation and increases in housing costs (DSS, 2000; Gordon, 2000). The latest evidence on the distribution of income for the 1998/99 financial year shows that the gap between rich and poor has continued to widen (Drever et al., 2000). Nevertheless, the overall rise in prosperity would make one expect that on average a greater proportion of people would consider common possessions and activities to be necessities in 1999 than in 1990 or 1983.

However, the results shown in Table 12 give a more complicated picture indicating that people's attitudes have been affected by changes in taste and technology as well as the growth in prosperity; the most substantial changes in attitudes are highlighted in bold. This table shows those items included in more than one of the surveys, most of them relating to adult necessities, but five relating to children that were already used in 1990.

Table 12: Proportions deeming items a necessity in 1999, 1990 and 1983

Item	1999	1990	1983
(bold type indicates changes of at least 10 percentage points in the 1990s)			
Damp-free home	94	98	96
Inside toilet		97	96
Heating to warm living areas of the home	95	97	97
Beds and bedding for everyone	95	97	97
Bath not shared		95	94
Money to keep home in a decent state of decoration	83	92	
Refrigerator	89	92	77
Warm, waterproof coat	87	91	87
Three meals a day for children	91	90	82
Two meals a day for adults	91	90	64
Insurance of contents of dwelling	80	88	
Fresh fruit and vegetables daily	87	88	
Toys (e.g. dolls, teddies)	84	84	71
Separate bedrooms for children aged 10 and over	80	82	77
Carpets in living rooms and bedrooms	**68**	**78**	**70**
Meat, fish or vegetarian equivalent every other day	81	77	63
Celebrations on special occasions	83	74	69
Two pairs of all-weather shoes	67	74	78
Washing machine	77	73	67
Presents for friends/family yearly	**58**	**69**	**63**
Out-of-school activities		69	
Regular savings (of £10 per month) for rainy days or retirement	67	68	
Hobby or leisure activity	**79**	**67**	**64**
New, not second-hand, clothes	**50**	**65**	**64**
Roast joint/vegetarian equivalent once a week	58	64	67
Leisure equipment	62	61	57
Television	58	58	51
Telephone	**72**	**56**	**43**
Holiday away from home once a year not with relatives	56	54	63
An outfit for social occasions	53	54	48
Outing for children weekly		53	40
Children's friends round for tea/snack fortnightly	59	52	37
Dressing gown	37	42	38
An evening out once a fortnight	41	42	36
Coach/train fares to visit friends/family quarterly	41	39	
Special lessons		39	
Friends or family round for a meal	**65**	**37**	**32**
Car	**36**	**26**	**22**
Pack of cigarettes		18	14
A meal in a restaurant/pub monthly	**27**	**17**	
Holidays abroad once a year	20	17	
Video cassette recorder	19	13	

Table 12 Continued

Item	1999	1990	1983
(bold type indicates changes of at least 10 percentage points in the 1990s)			
Home computer	11	5	
Dishwasher	7	4	
Dictionary	55		
Replace or repair broken electrical goods	86		
Visits to friends or family	85		
Visiting friends or family in hospital	92		
Deep freezer/fridge freezer	*55*		
Microwave	24		
Mobile phone	8		
Tumble dryer	20		
Satellite TV	5		
CD player	12		
Appropriate clothes for job interviews	70		
Medicines prescribed by doctor	91		
Access to the Internet	6		
A small amount of money to spend on self weekly	61		
Having a daily newspaper	32		
Going to the pub once a fortnight	22		
Attending weddings, funerals	81		
Attending place of worship	44		
Collect children from school	76		
Visits to school, e.g. sports day	81		

Some items that nearly all respondents felt to be necessary fluctuated by insignificant amounts in terms of the proportions considering them to be necessary between the three surveys. Three items – 'carpets in living rooms and bedrooms', 'presents for family/friends yearly' and 'new, not second-hand, clothes' – did fall substantially contrary to the expectation that as society got richer most items would be rated as necessities by more people. However, in most cases, asked about lower ranked, more luxury, items such as videos, dishwashers and cars, a greater proportion of respondents considered these to be necessities in 1999 than in 1990 or 1983. Similarly, many social and leisure activities such as 'celebrations on special occasions' and being able to afford a 'hobby or leisure activity' were thought to be a necessity by more respondents in 1999 than in the two previous surveys. This was also true for certain consumer durables such as telephones and washing machines. In particular there has been a remarkably rapid increase in the proportion of respondents that consider a telephone to be a necessity, from 43 per cent in 1983, to 56 per cent in 1990, to 72 per cent in 1999. Similarly 'friends or family round for a meal' increased from 37 per cent in 1990 to 64 per cent in 1999. However, this latter change may in part result from changes to the question wording (e.g. 1999 'friends or family round for a meal, snack or drink'; 1990 'friends/family round for a meal once a month').

Figure 4 compares the percentage of respondents who considered an item to be a necessity in 1999 (on the vertical axis) with the percentage of respondents in 1990 (horizontal axis), showing each item as a cross. If a line were to be drawn at a 45 degree angle from the bottom left to the top right of the chart, points lying on it would have had the same proportion of people citing them as necessities in

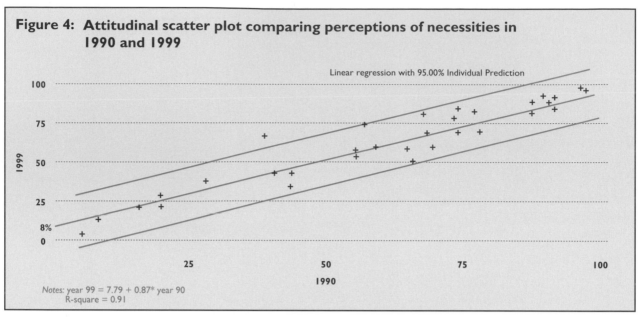

Figure 4: Attitudinal scatter plot comparing perceptions of necessities in 1990 and 1999

Linear regression with 95.00% Individual Prediction

1999

1990

Notes: year 99 = 7.79 + 0.87* year 90
R-square = 0.91

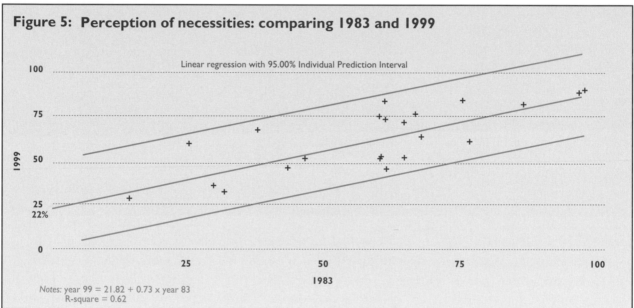

Figure 5: Perception of necessities: comparing 1983 and 1999

Linear regression with 95.00% Individual Prediction Interval

1999

1983

Notes: year 99 = 21.82 + 0.73 x year 83
R-square = 0.62

1990 and 1999. In fact there would be more items to the left/above this line and these had higher proportions citing them as necessities in 1999 than in 1990. A statistical technique can be used to 'fit' a line through the points that minimises the total distances between the line and individual items. This is the middle line on the diagram. It confirms that items considered to be important necessities by a large number of respondents in 1990 are also thought to be so by a large number of respondents in 1999.

It is difficult to interpret the line's slope, since it is affected by the fact that an item close to 100 per cent in 1990 cannot increase significantly by 1999. The

figure that therefore tells most about the change over time is the point at which the line intercepts one of the axes. This line crosses the 1999 axis at 8 per cent, showing that overall there was an 'average' 8 per cent increase in the public's perception of necessities between 1990 and 1999. This is as expected given the growth in average prosperity over the 1990s. Only those items that fall outside or close to the top and bottom solid lines show changes that are likely to be significantly different from the general trend.

Figure 5 shows that, between 1983 and 1999, there was an even larger shift in the public's perception of the necessities of life: a baseline increase of 22 per

Thatcher's children?

The possessions and activities highlighted in bold in Table 13 are those where there is a marked difference between the perceptions of the 16 to 24 age group in 1999, and both all adults in 1999 and the 16 to 24 age group in 1990. The table clearly shows that the 16 to 24 age group in 1999 considers that all clothing items are less important than do all adults in 1999 or did the 16 to 24 age group in 1990. Similarly, relatively few respondents in the 16 to 24 age group in 1999 thought 'insurance of contents of dwelling', 'fresh fruit and

vegetables daily', 'presents for friends/family yearly' and 'a roast joint/vegetarian equivalent once a week' were necessities. The consensus between age groups on the necessities of life, that all people in Britain should be able to afford and should not have to do without, appears to have weakened particularly in relation to basic clothing requirements. (However, as explained in Chapter 2 above, this still does not typically affect whether an item is considered a necessity by a majority among different groups, so the 'consensual' method of defining poverty used in this survey remains valid.)

Table 13: Proportion of 16- to 24-year-olds and all adults believing items to be necessities in 1990-99

Item	16 to 24 1999 (%)	16 to 24 1990 (%)	All adults 1999 (%)	All adults 1990 (%)
Damp-free home	94	95	94	98
Heating to warm living areas of the home	94	97	95	97
Beds and bedding for everyone	98	95	95	97
Money to keep home in a decent state of decoration	79	91	83	92
Refrigerator	92	92	89	92
Warm, waterproof coat	**79**	**85**	**87**	**91**
Three meals a day for children	94	93	91	90
Two meals a day for adults	97	95	91	90
Insurance of contents of dwelling	**71**	**87**	**80**	**88**
Fresh fruit and vegetables daily	**80**	**87**	**87**	**88**
Toys for children (e.g. dolls, teddies)	83	90	84	84
Separate bedrooms for children aged 10 and over	72	77	80	82
Carpets in living rooms and bedrooms	68	82	68	78
Meat, fish or vegetarian equivalent every other day	74	70	81	77
Celebrations on special occasions	86	77	83	74
Two pairs of all-weather shoes	**47**	**63**	**67**	**74**
Washing machine	68	68	77	73
Presents for friends/family yearly	**49**	**72**	**58**	**69**
Regular savings (of £10 per month) for rainy days or retirement	66	68	67	68
Hobby or leisure activity	80	67	79	67
New, not second-hand, clothes	**35**	**59**	**50**	**65**
Roast joint/vegetarian equivalent once a week	**34**	**55**	**58**	**64**
Leisure equipment	56	62	62	61
Television	**42**	**53**	**58**	**58**
Telephone	59	45	72	56
Holiday away from home once a year not with relatives	47	46	56	54

Table 13 Continued

Item	16 to 24 1999 (%)	16 to 24 1990 (%)	All adults 1999 (%)	All adults 1990 (%)
An outfit for social occasions	**45**	**54**	**53**	**54**
Children's friends round for tea/snack once a fortnight	61	50	59	52
Dressing gown	**16**	**24**	**37**	**42**
An evening out once a fortnight	48	50	41	42
Coach/train fares to visit friends/family quarterly	39	31	41	39
Friends or family round for a meal	61	35	65	37
Car	27	22	36	26
A meal in a restaurant/pub monthly	22	13	27	17
Holidays abroad once a year	20	23	20	17
Video casstte recorder	16	17	19	13
Home computer	13	4	11	5
Dishwasher	7	4	7	4

Note: Items in bold show marked difference between 16 to 24 age group in 1999 with the same group in 1990 and with all adults in 1999

Several commentators have remarked that the children who grew up knowing only Conservative governments may as adults have rather more 'conservative' views than their parents who grew up during the 1960s and 1970s. However, it must be noted that there has been little other than anecdotal evidence to support this view. An alternative interpretation of these data is that young people have become less materialistic.

Many young men and women suffered from profound socio-economic changes during the 1990s which resulted in fewer young people being employed in full-time jobs in 1999 than in 1990. Relative to older adults, the earnings and benefit rates for young people diminished. Larger numbers of young men and women now enter post-school education and training schemes than was the case in 1990. Although education and training improves long-term earnings prospects, it is associated with lower income in the short term. This relative impoverishment of youth may be as important a factor in explaining the change in attitudes amongst the younger cohort as any cultural effect of 18 years of Conservative rule. Young people in 1999 were almost twice as likely to be in education and training than in 1990 and students have always been more restricted in their perceptions of necessities than their working peers. Unfortunately, due to the differences between the surveys and changes in the definition of employment status (particularly for working students) it is not possible to quantify the relative importance of cultural changes compared with these socio-economic changes.

cent. This again reflects the large average increases in wealth experienced by the majority of the British population over this period.

Over the 16 years between 1983 and 1999, the British population has, as a whole, become more generous in what it considers to be necessities of life that everybody should be able to afford. As the average wealth of the population has increased and technology has progressed, so goods and services that were once luxuries have become more generally available and have begun to be perceived as necessities by increasing numbers of people.

However, the 1990s witnessed an apparent polarisation between the attitudes of the young (aged 16 to 24) and the rest of the population. The young have always made harsher judgements on what are necessities than older generations, but this became more pronounced between 1990 and 1999. This is discussed in the box on pages 47-8, and helps explain why there was not a simple pattern of all

Table 14: Changes in the perception of children's necessities between 1995 and 1999

Item	1999 All adults (%)	1999 Parents (%)	1995 Small Fortunes Survey (%)
Food			
Three meals a day	91	91	93
Fresh fruit or vegetables daily*	94	93	89
Meat, fish or vegetarian equivalent at least twice a day	77	76	68
Clothing			
Warm, waterproof coat‡	95	95	94
New, properly fitted, shoes	94	96	94
All required school uniform	88	88	79
4 jumpers/cardigans/sweatshirts	73	71	62
Some new, not second-hand, clothes	70	67	61
At least 7 pairs of new underpants	83	84	59
At least 4 pairs of trousers	69	74	59
Participation and activities			
Celebrations on special occasions	93	92	74
Hobby or leisure activity	90	88	66
School trip at least once a term	74	73	50
Holiday away from home at least one week a year	71	63	47
Swimming at least once a month	78	71	40
Friends round for tea/snack fortnightly	59	53	**
Leisure equipment	60	57	33
Development			
Books of own	89	90	82
Play group at least once a week (pre-school age children)	88	89	74
Educational games	83	84	73
Toys (e.g. dolls, teddies)	84	85	66
Construction toys	62	66	46
Bike: new/second-hand	55	60	32
At least 50p per week for sweets	49	45	26
Computer suitable for schoolwork	42	38	20
Computer games	18	13	5
Environmental			
A bed and bedding for self	93	96	94
Garden to play in	69	68	70
Bedroom for every child of different sex over 10 years	78	77	69
Carpet in bedroom	67	75	62

Notes: * In Small Fortunes, the item parents were asked for their opinion on was 'fresh fruit once a day'
‡ In Small Fortunes, this item was identified as two separate items - 'warm coat' and 'waterproof coat'. The percentage given is for warm coat. The percentage of parents endorsing waterproof coat as a necessity was 80 per cent.
** This item was inadvertently omitted from the Small Fortunes Survey

items having a higher proportion of people thinking of them as necessities in 1999 than previously. If one excludes young adults, few items are considered necessities by a declining proportion.

Changes in perceptions of necessities for children

The measures of necessities in the original Breadline Britain study included only five items that were specifically for children and which can be used for comparison with the Omnibus Survey. However, it is possible to compare adult judgements about what are necessities for children in 1995 when the Small Fortunes Survey was undertaken (Middleton et al., 1997), and in 1999, using the ONS Omnibus Survey.

More adults in the 1999 Omnibus Survey were inclined to say that things were necessities for children than parents in the Small Fortunes Survey (Table 14). This was so for all adults and for parents, and for all items with the exception of 'three meals a day' and a 'garden to play in', where the differences were very small – one or two percentage points. Eight items were endorsed as necessities by less than half of parents in 1995. This was reduced to only three items by 1999.

With one or two exceptions, differences between the judgements of parents and adults as a whole in the 1999 survey were very small. Differences emerged for a 'holiday away from home once a year', which 8 per cent fewer parents thought was a necessity than all adults, and for a 'carpet in their bedroom' and 'swimming at least once a month', which 8 and 7 per cent more parents thought to be a necessity than all adults respectively. In Table 14 comparisons are made between parents in the Omnibus Survey and the Small Fortunes Survey parents, since the two samples are more directly comparable.

In general, the smallest increases in the percentage judging children's items and activities as necessary occurred for those items that already had very high levels of endorsement as necessary in the earlier survey. These are two of the three food items, 'new, properly fitted, shoes', and a bed and bedding of their own. Many of the largest increases occurred for items that encourage participation in the social

world of childhood – in particular, a 'hobby or leisure activity', 'leisure equipment', a 'school trip at least once a term', and 'swimming at least once a month' (all increases of over 20 per cent). Very large increases can also be seen in the group of items that contribute to children's social and educational development, particularly: 'toys (e.g. dolls, teddies)'; 'construction toys'; a 'new/second-hand bike'; and a 'computer suitable for schoolwork' (although this last item was still not regarded as necessary by the majority of parents in 1999). It seems that awareness of the importance of items to aid children's social participation and educational development is growing among parents.

However, despite this general trend towards higher percentage endorsement of necessities, parent's priorities for children remain much the same – the basic necessities of food, clothing and health are seen as more important than participation and development. Of the five items most frequently judged to be necessities in 1995, four of these items were still in this position in 1999: 'new, properly fitted shoes', own bed and bedding, a 'warm, waterproof coat' and 'fresh fruit or vegetables daily'. Of the five items that were least likely to be regarded as necessities in 1995, four were still in the bottom five in 1999: 'leisure equipment', 'at least 50p a week for sweets', 'computer suitable for schoolwork', and 'computer games'.

Changes in deprivation

As technology advances, items that were once expensive luxuries become cheaper to produce and can begin to be afforded by increasing sections of the population. Therefore, it would be expected that fewer and fewer people would suffer from not being able to afford individual items (whether they be luxuries or necessities) as time progressed since, in virtually every case, all these items have become relatively less expensive with time.

However, the results shown in Table 15 indicate that this process occurred with glacial slowness for poor people during the 1980s and has virtually ceased during the 1990s. The proportion of households that could not afford an item did not change overall between 1990 and 1999 and changed by only 0.5 per

Table 15: Households lacking items because they can't afford them: 1999, 1990 and 1983 compared

	1999 Don't have, can't afford (%)	1990 Don't have, can't afford (%)	1983 Don't have, can't afford (%)
Beds and bedding for everyone	1	1	1
Heating to warm living areas of the home	3	3	5
Damp-free home	6	2	7
Two meals a day	1	1	3
Refrigerator	*	1	2
Fresh fruit and vegetables daily	5	6	-
Warm, waterproof coat	4	4	7
Celebrations on special occasions	2	4	4
Money to keep home in a decent state of decoration	15	15	-
Meat, fish or vegetarian equivalent every other day	2	3	8
Insurance of contents of dwelling	10	10	-
Hobby or leisure activity	7	6	7
Washing machine	2	4	6
Telephone	2	7	11
Carpets in living rooms and bedrooms	2	2	2
Regular savings (of £10 per month) for rainy days or retirement	27	30	-
Two pairs of all-weather shoes	7	5	9
Friends or family round for a meal	6	10	11
Television	*	1	*
Roast joint/vegetarian equivalent once a week	4	6	7
Presents for friends/family yearly	4	5	5
Holiday away from home once a year not with relatives	18	20	21
An outfit for social occasions	5	8	10
New, not second-hand, clothes	6	4	6
Car	*11*	*18*	*22*
Coach/train fares to visit friends/family quarterly	*19*	*19*	*-*
An evening out once a fortnight	*17*	*14*	*17*
Dressing gown	*1*	*2*	*3*
A meal in a restaurant/pub monthly	*21*	*22*	*-*
Video cassette recorder	*2*	*11*	*-*
Holidays abroad once a year	*29*	*32*	*-*
Home computer	*17*	*16*	*-*
Dishwasher	*11*	*18*	*-*

Note: * less than 0.5%

Items not considered necessities by a majority of the population in any year shown in italics cent between 1983 and 1999 (in the sense that if a scatter diagram similar to Figures 4 and 5 was drawn, the 'fitted' line would cross the 1999 axis at 0.5). The majority of this small change was accounted for by 'luxury' items (video, dishwasher, car, etc.) becoming relatively cheaper over the past 17 years. The only item considered to be a necessity by a majority of the population for which there was a big drop was the telephone – with only 2 per cent unable to afford one in 1999 compared with 7 per cent in 1990 and 11 per cent in 1983 (when only a minority considered it a necessity).

In the case of several necessities shown in Table 15, deprivation rose between 1990 and 1999. The number of households unable to afford a 'damp-free home', 'two pairs of all-weather shoes' and 'new, not second-hand clothes' all increased. In each case this rise followed a fall in the 1980s. The long-term health consequences of damp housing are now well documented. Children who suffered from multiple housing deprivation are 25 per cent more likely to become seriously ill by the age of 33 than the rest of the population after allowing for other major causes of ill health (Marsh et al., 1999).

Slightly, fewer households could afford a home computer in 1999 than in 1990 despite the huge fall in the price of computers in real terms over the 1990s. This is a disturbing finding given that the importance of the Internet is likely to increase during the twenty-first century. The Government is attempting to ensure universal access, so that British society does not become divided into the 'information poor' and 'information rich'.

Changes in poverty

There are a number of differences between the previous 1983 and 1990 Breadline Britain surveys and the current PSE survey that make direct comparison difficult. The PSE survey is much more accurate and detailed (and more expensive), which allowed detailed information on poverty, social exclusion and low income to be collected at the individual level, whereas the Breadline Britain surveys collected information at the household level and only had limited information about income.

This section compares the changes in poverty and deprivation between 1983 and 1999, using the somewhat cruder methods and definitions of poverty and deprivation that were available in 1983, so that the results are directly comparable. Thus in order to produce directly comparable data across time poverty has been defined at the household level as lacking three or more items considered by the population to be necessities due to insufficient income.

This procedure slightly underestimates the 'true' amount of poverty discussed in Chapter 2.[2] Two differences in this cruder definition are, first of all that it does not include people who lack two rather than three items, and second that it does include people currently deprived of necessities, but whose relatively high income indicates that they have recently risen out of poverty. There is also a difference from the measure used in Chapter 2 because of the need to look at households when measuring poverty over time: the 1999 measure of individual poverty was not possible from the data in previous surveys.

Between 1983 and 1990, the number of *households* who lacked three or more socially perceived necessities increased by almost 50 per cent. In 1983, 14 per cent of households were living in poverty, and by 1990 this figure was 21 per cent. Poverty continued to increase during the 1990s and, by 1999, the number of households living in poverty on this definition had again increased to over 24 per cent, approximately 1 in 4 households.

Thus, just as poverty measured by income inequality has risen over the past two decades (see Figure 1, page 8), so poverty measured by the enforced deprivation of necessities has increased - by an average rate of 1 per cent of households per year during the 1980s and at a slower average rate of 0.3 per cent of households per year during the 1990s. This represented about half a million extra people living in poverty on average each year between 1983 and 1990, and a smaller but continuing increase during the 1990s. This dramatic rise in poverty, in terms of the enforced lack of necessities, occurred while the majority of the British population became richer.

THE GROWTH OF POVERTY IN BRITAIN

Table 16: Long-term chronic poverty in 1990 and 1999

	Households in 1990 (%)	Households in 1999 (%)
Not poor	79.0	76.0
Poor (not long-term)	17.0	21.5
Long-term poor	4.0	2.5

Long-term poverty

Although poverty affects a quarter of British households, in the majority of cases the welfare state provides an effective 'safety net' which prevents people from sinking too deeply into poverty. For many households, the experience of poverty is extremely unpleasant but relatively brief. It is possible to estimate from the PSE survey the number of households that suffer from long-term chronic poverty. The 1990 Breadline Britain survey showed that these households invariably suffered from extremes of multiple deprivation, misery and want.

This 'long-term poor' group was defined in 1990 as households who have a deprivation score of three or more (objective poverty), who consider that they are genuinely poor 'all the time' (subjective poverty) and who have lived in poverty in the past either 'often' or 'most of the time' (persistent poverty).

Just over 4 per cent of households were long-term poor in 1990. However, this had fallen to 2.5 per cent of households by 1999 (Table 16). Thus, although more than half a million households were suffering from long-term chronic poverty in 1999, the numbers have fallen over the 1990s. Whilst there were more poor households at the end of the 1990s than there were at the beginning of the decade, there were fewer households suffering from chronic long-term poverty in 1999, according to the comparative measure we have used, than in 1990.

The implications for policy of this evidence of growing poverty are considerable. To halt and reverse the trend as the Government has committed itself to doing will require major structural actions affecting benefits, taxes, public services, market conditions and earnings. These implications will be examined in detail in subsequent reports.

Notes

1 Source: Institute for Fiscal Studies database

2 The improvements to the measurement of poverty in the PSE survey are evolutionary compared with the Breadline Britain methods. There is nothing radically wrong with what was done in the 1983 and 1990 surveys and, indeed, the directly comparable data produced in Chapter 4 tells a very similar story. The 1983 and 1990 results should not be thought of as wrong any more than the HBAI is wrong because of the inadequacies of the McClements' equivalisation scale. There is always room for improvement and that is what the PSE represents.

Social exclusion in Britain

The PSE survey distinguishes between four dimensions of exclusion: impoverishment, or exclusion from adequate income or resources; labour market exclusion; service exclusion; and exclusion from social relations. The first of these aspects, poverty itself, is covered in the rest of this report. The present chapter sets out the main findings of the survey in relation to the other three dimensions, with particular emphasis on exclusion from social relations. Exploration of this last aspect is unique to the PSE survey and is generally neglected in approaches that rely on proxy indicators. Subsequent analyses, to be published separately, will explore the relationships between the dimensions of exclusion.

Exclusion from the labour market

Because General Household Survey data are available for all respondents to the PSE, we can look at both individual and household exclusion from the labour market.

Individual and household exclusion are important for different reasons. Individual attachment to the labour market is increasingly held to be important not just because it is a route to an adequate income, but because paid work is seen as an important arena of social contact and social interaction. Individuals not in paid work may therefore be held to be socially excluded, whether or not they live with other adults in paid work and whether or not the household is poor.

However, not being in paid work may also lead to poverty, service exclusion and exclusion from social relations, and this may be more likely to happen to individuals in households with no adult in paid work. These households are sometimes referred to as 'workless households'. However, many of them

Table 17: Labour market participation by age, gender and health status (percentage)

	Economic status of respondent						
	Working	Un-employed	Permanently unable to work	Retired	Domestic and caring activities	Student	Other inactive
Age of respondent							
16-34	76	6	1	0	8	8	0
35-54	80	4	6	1	7	1	2
55-64	38	2	15	33	8	0	4
65+	7		1	85	5	0	2
Sex							
Male	63	4	6	21	2	3	1
Female	50	3	4	26	12	3	2
Has long-standing illness							
No	69	4	0	16	7	3	1
Yes	35	3	13	37	7	2	3
Total	**57**	**3**	**5**	**24**	**7**	**3**	**2**

include people doing large amounts of unpaid work caring for children or adult dependants, so they are better described as 'jobless households'. For similar reasons, the following account uses the term 'labour market inactive' for those neither in paid work nor unemployed on an ILO definition, in place of the more conventional but misleading 'economically inactive'.

Table 17 shows the extent of labour market participation by age group, gender and health status. The results show that 43 per cent of adults (50 per cent of women and 37 per cent of men) have no paid work. Overall, 3 per cent (4 per cent of men and 3 per cent of women) are unemployed but the majority of those not in paid work are 'labour market inactive'. Many of these are people over working age and, in all, more than half of them describe themselves as retired. However, non-participation in paid work is by no means confined to those over pensionable age. In the 55 to 64 age group, 62 per cent are not in paid work. While about half of these describe themselves as retired, a substantial proportion (15 per cent) are sick or disabled, or are engaged in domestic and caring activities (8 per cent). These last two are the main reasons for labour market inactivity in younger age groups, with caring responsibilities at least six times as likely to take

women out of paid employment as men. Disability is a major correlate of labour market inactivity. Those with long-standing illness are about half as likely to be in paid work and more than twice as likely to be labour market inactive, than those without.

Overall, the data suggest that we should be cautious about treating labour market inactivity in itself as social exclusion, since it affects a very high proportion of the population. However, in so far as it may be a risk factor, we should be alert to its distribution and to its correlation with more direct indicators of exclusion.

Living in a jobless household is often taken as an indicator of social exclusion. Table 18 shows that, overall, over 1 in 3 of the population lives either in a pensioner household (21 per cent) or in a jobless non-pensioner household (13 per cent). Nearly two-fifths of individuals (38 per cent) living in non-pensioner jobless households are aged between 55 and 64; one-third of all people in this age group (33 per cent) live in jobless households. Among younger people, about 1 in 8 of those aged 16 to 34, and 1 in 10 of those aged 35 to 54 are in households with no paid work. Women are more likely than men to live in pensioner or jobless non-pensioner

Table 18: Workers in household (percentage of respondents)

	Workers in household		
	No workers (%)	Workers (%)	Retired (%)
Age of respondent			
16-34	13	87	
35-54	10	90	
55-64	33	56	11
65+	5	6	89
Sex			
Male	13	70	17
Female	14	62	24
Has long-standing illness			
No	9	77	14
Yes	20	47	32
Total	**13**	**66**	**21**

households. Those with long-standing illness are one and a half times as likely as others to live in households without paid work.

Service exclusion

One aspect of social exclusion is lack of access to basic services, whether in the home (such as power and water supplies) or outside it (such as transport, shopping facilities and financial services).

Utility disconnections constitute exclusion from basic domestic services which most people take for granted. We asked about disconnections of water, gas, electricity and telephone and whether people had restricted their use of these services because of cost. The answers are presented in Table 19. Six per cent had experienced disconnection from one or more services and 11 per cent had used less than they needed because they were unable to afford them ('restricted consumption'). Both disconnection and restricted consumption declined with age. Women were slightly more likely than men to have experienced disconnection and were nearly twice as likely to have restricted consumption. Households with children were at greater risk on both counts. Those with long-standing illness were less likely than others to have been disconnected but much more likely to have restricted consumption. Those in non-pensioner jobless households were nearly four times as likely to have restricted consumption and nearly three times as likely as those in households with paid work to have been disconnected (31 per cent and 14 per cent, compared with 8 per cent and 5 per cent).

Respondents were asked about access to a range of public services (e.g. libraries, hospitals and post offices) and private services (e.g. corner shops, banks and pubs) outside the home (Table 21). In each case, they were asked whether they used the service, used it but considered it inadequate, did not use it and did not want to, did not use it because it was unavailable, or did not use it because they could not afford to. This enabled us to differentiate between 'collective exclusion', where services are simply not available or unsuitable and 'individual exclusion', where they are priced out of individual reach. Overall, 24 per cent were excluded from two or more

Table 19: Utility disconnections and restricted use experienced by respondents		
	Has experienced disconnection (%)	Has restricted consumption (%)
Age of respondent		
16-34	10	13
35-54	7	12
55-64	1	10
65+	1	6
Sex		
Male	5	8
Female	6	13
Has long-standing illness		
No	6	7
Yes	5	17
Household type		
Single	3	13
Couple	3	8
Household with children	7	15
Other	9	8
Workers in household		
No worker	14	31
Workers	5	8
Retired	1	7
Economic status of respondent		
Working	5	7
Unemployed	20	33
Labour market inactive	5	13
Total	**6**	**11**

services because they were either unaffordable or unavailable. Only 54 per cent of the population have access to the full range of publicly and privately provided services.

For both publicly and privately provided services, lack of availability rather than lack of affordability is the main barrier to use. Lack of availability, or

Table 20: Respondents lacking different numbers of services because unaffordable and/or unavailable

	Number of services lacking		
	I (%)	2 or more (%)	Total (%)
Public services			
Cannot afford	3	I	4
Unavailable	20	8	28
Cannot afford or unavailable	21	10	31
Private services			
Cannot afford	4	2	6
Unavailable	15	11	26
Cannot afford or unavailable	16	14	30
Both public and private			
Cannot afford	5	4	9
Unavailable	23	18	41
Cannot afford or unavailable	22	24	46

'collective exclusion', affects nearly one-third of respondents for both public and private services. The level of collective exclusion from adequate services is, however, higher, since substantial proportions who use individual services regard these services as inadequate. Lack of affordability, or 'individual exclusion', affected only 1 in 10. The main items for which charges were cited as a deterrent were evening classes and visits to the pub or cinema/theatre (Table 21). There are small numbers of respondents who do not have access to the basic health services of opticians because of cost. Access to public transport is problematic for a significant minority of the population - 6 per cent cited bus services as unavailable or unsuitable, and 11 per cent were unable to use train services because they were either unavailable or unaffordable. A further 15 per cent regarded bus services and 10 per cent, train services, as unavailable. These figures are likely to be underestimates rather than overestimates of both collective and individual exclusion, since some people prefer to say that they do not want services than to admit that they cannot afford them.

Table 22 shows the characteristics of those who lack at least two services because they are either unaffordable and/or unavailable. The major

difference is that 33 per cent of people in non-pensioner jobless households lack access to two or more services compared with 21 per cent of those with workers, and 30 per cent of unemployed or not-working respondents lack this access compared to 20 per cent of those in work. A similar difference in access is apparent in comparing those having a long-standing illness with those that do not (30 per cent to 21 per cent). There is a smaller increased risk if you are a woman (27 per cent compared with 20 per cent for men). These groups with an increased probability of lacking services are similar whether one is considering private or public services.

In terms of lacking access to two or more services overall (Table 22), those aged over 65 have a higher risk (29 per cent, compared with 21 per cent for those aged 35 to 64). However, further analysis showed, while exclusion from two or more private services is more common among those aged over 65, exclusion from two or more public services declines slightly with age, so that this group has rather better access than the rest of the population. The probable explanation for this is that public services are generally provided free or cheaply to those over 65, suggesting that the Welfare State does work and that the best way of delivering services to vulnerable

Table 21: Which public and private services respondents used

	Use - adequate (%)	Collective exclusion		Individual exclusion	
		Use - inadequate (%)	Don't use - unavailable or unsuitable (%)	Don't use – can't afford (%)	Don't use – don't want or not relevant (%)
Public services					
Libraries	55	6	3	0	36
Public sports facilities	39	7	5	1	48
Museums and galleries	29	4	13	1	52
Evening classes	17	2	5	3	73
A public or community village hall	31	3	9	0	56
A hospital with accident/ emergency unit	75	13	2	0	10
Doctor	92	6	0	0	2
Dentist	83	5	1	0	11
Optician	78	3	1	1	17
Post office	93	4	0	0	2
Private services					
Places of worship	30	1	2	0	66
Bus services	38	15	6	0	41
Train or tube station	37	10	10	1	41
Petrol stations	75	2	2	1	21
Chemist	93	3	1	0	3
Corner shop	73	7	8	0	12
Medium to large supermarket	92	4	2	0	2
Banks or building societies	87	7	1	0	4
Pub	53	4	2	2	37
Cinema or theatre	45	6	10	5	33

groups is by providing public services, free at the point of use.

Referring to Table 21, among the services asked about were banks and building societies. Five per cent of adults said they did not use these services. In most cases, the reason given was that they did not want to. Whilst 1 per cent said they were unavailable, none said that they could not afford them. Lack of access to a bank account is an increasingly important marker of financial exclusion, as fewer and fewer transactions can be effected purely in cash and as the provision of post offices and sub-post offices declines. The question about access to services was supplemented by a direct question about the possession of bank or building society accounts. Seven per cent of adults have no access to a bank account in their own right. About 1 in 4 of these lives with a partner or spouse with an account but 1 in 20 of the household population appear to be currently without access to one, either personally or by proxy.

It is important to note that factors other than price may also result in effective exclusion from services and activities. Those with limiting long-standing illness or disability were asked about difficulties in accessing various services. Nearly 1 in 3 reported great difficulty using services such as cinemas, museums, shops and restaurants and 1 in 6 had had

Table 22: Service exclusion by selected key variables

	Number of public/private services unaffordable/unavailable		
	1 (%)	2 or more (%)	Total (%)
Age of respondent			
16-34	16	26	42
35-54	27	21	49
55-64	21	19	40
65+	23	29	52
Sex			
Male	22	20	42
Female	22	27	49
Has long-standing illness			
No	22	21	43
Yes	22	30	52
Household type			
Single	20	29	49
Couple	21	25	46
Household with children	24	21	45
Other	22	22	44
Workers in household			
No worker	19	33	52
Workers	22	21	43
Retired	23	27	51
Economic status of respondent			
Working	22	20	42
Unemployed	15	30	45
Labour market inactive	22	30	52
Total	**22**	**24**	**46**

Note: Numbers may not sum due to rounding

problems arranging accommodation or insurance or using banks, building societies and public telephones (Table 23).

Exclusion from social relations

A unique feature of the PSE survey is that it seeks direct information about social relations and social participation. At this stage of the analysis, we can simply describe the pattern of exclusion from social relations among the household population. In future analysis, the links between this and other aspects of exclusion - poverty, joblessness and service exclusion - can be explored. Exclusion from social relations can be looked at in different ways: through non-participation in common social activities; isolation; lack of support; disengagement; and confinement.

Non-participation in common social activities
Tables 24 and 25 show the extent to which people participate in a range of common social activities and the proportion excluded by lack of money. Only

Table 23: Activity/service difficulty due to health problem or disability

	Access difficult due to health problem or disability (%)
Activity	
Go to the cinema, theatre or concerts	15
Go to the library, art galleries or museums	9
Go shopping	15
Eat out in a restaurant or have a drink	11
Go to a football match or other sporting event	10
Other	7
Have had no great difficulty in doing these things	71
Service	
Arrange accommodation in a hotel or boarding house	4
Arrange insurance	6
Use a bank or building society	4
Use a public telephone	4
Other	2
Have had no great difficulty in using these services	86

63 per cent of the population can afford the full range of social activities (this includes some items, shown in italics, that are not considered necessities by the majority, as this section is about social exclusion, not poverty). One in 10 of the population is excluded by lack of money from participation in five or more social activities, 20 per cent from three or more, and 27 per cent from two or more. Holidays, going out and eating out are the activities which are most curtailed by lack of money, but 6 per cent of the population said they were unable to have

Table 24: Number of common social activities that cannot be afforded

	(%)	Cumulative (%)
1	11	73
2	7	80
3/4	10	90
5 or more	10	100
Total	**100**	**100**

Note: Columns may not sum due to rounding

Table 25: Participation in common social activities

	Essential (%)	Do activity (%)	Don't do/ don't want (%)	Don't do/ can't afford (%)
Visiting friends or family in hospital	92	88	9	3
Visits to friends or family	84	95	3	2
Celebrations on special occasions	83	96	2	2
Visits to school, e.g. sports day	81	52	46	3
Attending weddings, funerals	80	94	3	3
Hobby or leisure activity	78	81	12	7
Collect children from school	75	45	52	3
Friends or family round for a meal	64	84	10	6
Holiday away from home once a year	55	68	14	18
Attending place of worship	41	31	68	1
An evening out once a fortnight	39	61	23	16
Coach/train fares to visit friends/family quarterly	38	30	55	18
A meal in a restaurant/pub monthly	26	60	21	19
Going to the pub once a fortnight	20	47	43	10
Holidays abroad once a year	19	48	25	28

Note: Items in italics were not considered to be necessities by more than 50% of the population

Table 26: Non-participation in common social activities because respondents cannot afford them, by selected variables

	Social activities lacking because cannot afford				
	1 (%)	2 (%)	3/4 (%)	5+ (%)	Total (%)
Age of respondent					
16-34	13	9	11	16	49
35-54	10	4	11	10	36
55-64	9	4	9	7	29
65+	9	9	8	5	31
Sex					
Male	11	7	8	9	36
Female	10	6	11	12	39
Has long-standing illness					
No	12	7	9	9	37
Yes	8	7	11	13	38
Household type					
Single	10	6	10	10	35
Couple	9	5	6	5	25
Household with children	13	9	15	16	53
Other	11	6	9	12	38
Workers in household					
No worker	10	9	14	28	60
Workers	11	6	9	8	35
Retired	8	8	9	6	32
Economic status of respondent					
Working	12	6	8	8	34
Unemployed	6	6	21	32	65
Labour market inactive	9	8	12	12	40
Total	**11**	**7**	**10**	**10**	**37**

friends or family round for a meal, snack or drink. Seven per cent were unable to afford a hobby or leisure activity. Smaller numbers were excluded from such basic social activities as visiting family and friends, even when in hospital, and attending weddings and funerals.

Table 26 shows the groups participating in social activities. Most strikingly, these are unemployed people (59 per cent, compared with 23 per cent of working people) and those living in jobless non-

pensioner households (51 per cent compared with 23 per cent of people in households with workers or pensioners). There is also lower participation by households with children (40 per cent compared with 26 per cent of single people and 16 per cent of couples without children). Greater proportions of the youngest age group (aged 16 to 34) lack participation in two or more activities (36 per cent compared with 25 per cent of those aged 35 to 54, and 20 per cent or more of those aged 55 and over). A slightly higher proportion of women do not participate in two or

Table 27: Factors preventing participation in common social activities

	Non-participation (%)
Can't afford to	47
Not interested	44
Lack of time due to childcare responsibilities	18
Too old, ill, sick or disabled	14
Lack of time due to paid work	14
No one to go out with (social)	6
No vehicle/poor public transport	5
Lack of time due to other caring responsibilities	4
Fear of burglary or vandalism	3
Fear of personal attack	3
Can't go out due to other caring responsibilities	2
Problems with physical access	1
Feel unwelcome (e.g. due to disability, ethnicity, gender, age, etc.)	1
None of these	8

Note: Multiple responses allowed

more activities (29 per cent compared with 24 per cent of men). Lack of money is not the only factor preventing people from participating in the listed activities, although it is cited more often than any other, closely followed by lack of interest. Table 27 summarises the range of other reasons given, including principally lack of time due to childcare and other caring responsibilities, sickness and disability, and lack of time due to paid work. This last factor suggests caution in treating labour market activity as a simple route to social inclusion even for those of working age, and requires further exploration.

Isolation

Respondents were asked about the frequency with which they saw or spoke to family members or friends outside their immediate household, including both face-to-face and telephone contact. Table 28 shows that over half the population (59 per cent) have at least one non-household family member whom they see or speak to on a daily basis. Daily

contact is higher for the 55 to 64 age group, for women, for those living in non-pensioner jobless households and those not in paid work. It is notable that those in non-pensioner jobless households have more frequent family contact than those in households with paid work. Most people (91 per cent) have non-household family members with whom they have some contact at least weekly and only 1 per cent has no family contact at least a few times a year.

More than 1 in 4 (28 per cent) has no friend with whom they are in contact on a daily basis. Only 8 per cent have no friend with whom they are in contact at least weekly. A small minority (3 per cent) has no contact with friends even a few times a year. In terms of daily contact with friends, 37 per cent of those aged over 65 do not have this, compared with about 30 per cent of those aged 35 to 64 and less than 20 per cent of the youngest group (aged 16 to 34). Forty per cent of couple households do not have this daily contact with friends, compared with less than 25 per cent for other household types. Both pensioner and non-pensioner jobless households (64 per cent and 69 per cent respectively) are less likely to see friends on a daily basis than working households (76 per cent), but those who are unemployed are more likely to see friends daily (81 per cent) than those in work (75 per cent). However, those economically inactive fare worse than either (68 per cent). The pattern for those who do not have contact with any friends at least weekly is similar.

Looking at patterns of contact with either family or friends, 1 in 8 (13 per cent) have neither a family member nor a friend outside their household with whom they are in contact on a daily basis. Only 3 per cent had no weekly contact with a family member or friend and 2 per cent had no such contact even a few times a year. The groups most likely to be without daily contact are those over 65 (18 per cent compared with 9 per cent of those aged 16 to 34) and those living as couples (19 per cent compared with about 10 per cent for other household types).

The data on isolation in terms of contact with either friends or family show no difference between those

Table 28: Level of respondents' social contact with family and friends

	Contact with family and friends					
	Family		Friends		Family/friends	
	Daily	Weekly	Daily	Weekly	Daily	Weekly
	(%)	(%)	(%)	(%)	(%)	(%)
Age of respondent						
16-34	63	94	81	97	91	98
35-54	53	88	72	93	87	96
55-64	68	93	70	88	90	95
65+	58	90	63	90	82	97
Sex						
Male	51	89	68	91	85	96
Female	67	93	76	94	90	98
Has long-standing illness						
No	58	91	74	94	88	97
Yes	61	92	69	90	87	97
Household type						
Single	58	91	76	93	90	96
Couple	59	93	60	88	81	97
Household with children	59	90	79	96	92	97
Other	61	89	78	93	89	96
Workers in household						
No worker	71	94	69	90	89	97
Workers	57	90	76	94	88	97
Retired	58	91	64	90	83	97
Economic status of respondent						
Working	56	90	75	94	88	96
Unemployed	67	88	81	95	94	98
Labour market inactive	64	93	68	90	87	97
Total	**59**	**91**	**72**	**92**	**87**	**97**

in work and those economically inactive, while those who are unemployed are a little more likely to have daily contact with family and friends. Those living in jobless households are slightly less likely to lack social contacts than those in households with paid work. It appears, therefore, that joblessness for individuals and households does not necessarily increase social isolation in these terms. The reasons given for people not seeing family and friends more

often also suggest that paid work can contribute to this. The two most frequently cited reasons were distance and lack of time due to paid work.

Lack of support

One indicator of the existence of functioning social relationships and networks is the amount of practical and emotional support potentially available to individuals in times of need. Respondents were

Table 29: Number of situations in which respondents reported 'a lot of', or 'some' support

Number of situations in which potential support available	(%)
7	54
6	9
5	8
4	6
3	12
2	2
1	8
0	1
Total	**100**

Table 30: Proportion of respondents having potential support in each of seven situations

Type of support	'None'/ 'Not much'	'Some'/ 'A lot'
Informal caring	29	71
Help with relationship problems	23	77
Help with heavy household jobs	13	87
Advice	13	87
Looking after personal possessions	11	89
Talking to if depressed	11	89
Home help during personal illness	9	91

Table 31: Levels of overall support across all key areas by selected variables

	Level of support		
	Good	Reasonable	Poor
Age of respondent			
16-34	61	20	19
35-54	54	24	23
55-64	46	25	29
65+	48	28	24
Sex			
Male	51	23	26
Female	56	24	20
Has long-standing illness			
No	54	23	23
Yes	52	25	23
Household type			
Single	42	32	27
Couple	53	21	26
Household with children	61	23	16
Other	54	23	23
Workers in household			
No worker	47	33	20
Workers	56	21	23
Retired	49	27	25
Economic status of respondent			
Working	58	21	21
Unemployed	45	31	24
Labour market inactive	48	27	25

asked how much support they would expect to get in seven situations, including support from members of the household, other family and friends and any other means of support. Four items related to practical support: needing help around the home when in bed with flu; help with heavy household or gardening jobs; help with caring responsibilities for children or elderly or disabled adults; someone to look after the home or possessions when away. Three related to emotional support: needing advice about an important life change; someone to talk to if depressed; and someone to talk to about problems with a spouse or partner. The results are summarised in Table 29.

Only just over half (54 per cent) of the population expect to be able to call on 'some' or 'a lot' of support in all seven categories. More than 1 in 5 (23 per cent) lacks adequate support in at least four out of seven areas. Nearly 10 per cent have some or a lot of support in no situations or only one situation.

Table 30 shows that, in each situation, the majority of the population think they could rely on support but at least 1 in 10 have little or no support in each situation and this rises to about 1 in 4 in the case of advice about relationship problems and 1 in 3 for informal caring.

Those with 'thin' support (i.e. none or not much support) are not evenly spread through the population (Table 31). We divided the data into those with good support (some or a lot of support in all seven situations), reasonable support (lacking good support in one to three situations) and poor support (lacking good support in four or more situations). Overall, men have poorer support networks than women. People with jobs are more likely to expect good support than those unemployed or outside the labour market. Those in retired and non-pensioner jobless households report less supportive networks. However, those in non-pensioner jobless households are less likely to report poor, rather than reasonable, support than those in either retired or working households. It should be stressed that the questions asked were about help potentially available. They thus reflect how supported people feel, rather than being a simple measure of how supported they actually are - although of course respondents will also have drawn on their experience of support or the lack of it in specific situations. The higher expectations of those in paid work may not be wholly born out in practice.

Disengagement

Lack of civic engagement is sometimes deemed to be an important aspect of social exclusion. Respondents were asked which of a list of activities they had done in the last three years and whether they were currently actively involved in any of a comprehensive range of organisations. About 17 per cent have taken no such action at all in the previous three years. The only two activities which drew more than 1 in 3 of the population were voting in local and in general elections (Table 32).

Looking next at current participation in various types

of civic organisation, this revealed that just under 60 per cent are involved, with sports clubs claiming the highest number of participants, at around 18 per cent (Table 33). Combining the activities and organisations covered in Tables 32 and 33, a total of 88 per cent of individuals were engaged in some way, leaving just under 12 per cent apparently disengaged. The importance of voting in this total should be emphasised - excluding it would mean that 30 per cent are disengaged (Table 34).

The distribution of disengagement among different groups is also outlined in Table 34. With some exceptions, the patterns are similar for the 12 per cent who have no engagement at all and the 30 per cent who have no engagement beyond possibly voting. The differences between different groups are generally quite small. The 16-34 age group have relatively high levels of disengagement, compared with 35- to 64-year-olds, although it rises again to similar levels to the young for older people, apart from voting. Not working or being in a workless household tends to raise disengagement, although again retired households vote more.

Confinement

Participation in social activities and social contact beyond the household depends on being able to get out and about. People who are not able to move about freely may be effectively excluded from full social participation. In addition to factors such as affordability, childcare responsibilities, being too old, disabled or sick, or lack of time due to paid work (Table 27), other factors are involved which leave people substantially confined to their home and, in less extreme cases, reduce their level of activity. A prime example is personal safety. Table 35 shows that 30 per cent of the population feels unsafe walking alone after dark. Those most likely to feel unsafe are women, older people, those not in paid work and those in pensioner and non-pensioner jobless households (Table 35).

Table 32: Civic activities undertaken in the last three years

Activity	(%)
Voted in the last general election	73
Voted in the last local election	65
Helped on fundraising drives	29
Urged someone outside the family to vote	20
Presented views to local councillor	16
Urged someone to get in touch with a local councillor	16
Been an officer of an organisation or club	14
Made a speech before an organised group	11
Written a letter to an editor	5
Taken an active part in a political campaign	3
Stood for civic office	1
None of these	17

Note: Multiple responses allowed

Table 33: Current active involvement in civic organisations

Type of group	(%)
Sports club	18
Religious group or church organisation	12
Any other group or organisation	11
Trade union	10
Social club or working men's club	10
Tenants, Residents Association, Neighbourhood Watch	9
Voluntary service group	8
Parents' or school association	6
Environmental group	3
Other community or civic group	3
Women's group or organisation	3
Political party	2
Other pressure group	2
Women's Institute or Townswomen's Guild	1
None of these	41
Don't know	3

Note: Multiple responses allowed

Table 34: Respondents' lack of civic activity by selected variables

	Disengaged from activities (%)	Disengaged or only votes (%)
Age of respondent		
16-34	18	34
35-54	9	23
55-64	6	29
65+	11	34
Sex		
Male	13	30
Female	11	29
Has long-standing illness		
No	12	27
Yes	12	34
Household type		
Single	10	30
Couple	8	29
Household with children	12	27
Other	18	32
Workers in household		
No worker	17	35
Workers	12	27
Retired	9	35
Economic status of respondent		
Working	10	25
Unemployed	21	39
Labour market inactive	14	35
Total	**12**	**30**

Table 35: Respondents who feel safe or unsafe walking alone after dark, by selected variables

	Walking after dark	
	Feel safe (%)	Feel unsafe (%)
Age of respondent		
16-34	73	27
35-54	74	26
55-64	69	31
65+	62	38
Sex		
Male	83	17
Female	58	42
Has long-standing illness		
No	73	27
Yes	66	34
Household type		
Single	65	35
Couple	69	31
Household with children	76	24
Other	69	31
Workers in household		
No worker	64	36
Workers	75	25
Retired	61	39
Economic status of respondent		
Working	75	25
Unemployed	72	28
Labour market inactive	63	37
Total	**70**	**30**

Conclusion

There have been few previous attempts to operationalise the concept of social exclusion in empirical research. In this chapter we have explored three dimensions of social exclusion: exclusion from the labour market, service exclusion, and exclusion in social relations. In future work we will be exploring the interaction of these dimensions of social exclusion, and their interaction with the fourth dimension, poverty and impoverishment, using the battery of measures collected as part of the PSE survey. Through that analysis we hope to be able to establish the extent to which these dimensions are independent or associated with each other.

6 Conclusions

The Poverty and Social Exclusion Survey of Britain is the most comprehensive and scientifically rigorous survey of this type ever undertaken. It provides unparalleled detail about material and social deprivation and exclusion among the British population at the close of the twentieth century.

The UK Government and others have committed themselves to the aim of eliminating poverty throughout the world during the twenty-first century. The UK government has a key role to play not only by investigating and putting policies in place to reduce poverty but by influencing scientific standards of investigation, analysis of causes and reduction of poverty in other parts of the world. The PSE survey documents the scale and nature of the problem in Britain with regard to both poverty and social exclusion.

Poverty

By the end of 1999, approximately 14.5 million *people* (26 per cent) were living in poverty in Britain according to the PSE survey. The survey's measurement of poverty, by taking into account both low income and multiple deprivation of items socially defined as necessities, confirms that poverty rates have risen sharply since the early 1980s. Between 1983 and 1990, the number of households living in poverty increased by almost half – from 14 per cent to 21 per cent of the population. Poverty continued to increase during the 1990s and, by 1999, the number of *households* living in poverty had again increased, to over 24 per cent.

How does this figure compare to historic poverty levels? At times in the past, bigger proportions of the British population have been poor and their poverty has often been more severe and life-threatening. However, because of the growth in the size of the population in the twentieth century, a larger number of people in Britain today are poor, by the standards of the time, than was the case in previous centuries. The fact that an unprecedented absolute number of individuals are affected has significant implications for the scale and design of solutions.

The survey allows poverty to be described not just as an aggregate statistic but also in terms of the real conditions that people face. For example, out of 58 million people in Britain today:

- Roughly 9.5 million people in Britain cannot afford adequate housing conditions as perceived by the majority of the population. That is, they cannot afford to keep their home adequately heated, free from damp or in a decent state of decoration.[1]

- About 8 million people cannot afford one or more essential household goods, such as a fridge, a telephone or carpets for living areas, or to repair electrical goods or furniture when they break or wear out.

- Almost 7.5 million people are too poor to be able to engage in those common social activities considered necessary: visiting friends and family, attending weddings and funerals, or having celebrations on special occasions.

- A third of British children go without at least one of the things they need, like three meals a day, toys, out of school activities or adequate clothing. Eighteen per cent of children go without two or more items or activities defined as necessities by the majority of the population.

- About 6.5 million adults go without essential clothing, such as a warm waterproof coat, because of lack of money.

- Around 4 million people are not properly fed by today's standards. They do not have enough money to afford fresh fruit and vegetables, or two meals a day, for example.

- Over 10.5 million people suffer from financial insecurity. They cannot afford to save, insure their house contents or spend even small amounts of money on themselves.

Poverty appears to have become more widespread but not deepened over the 1990s. Between 1990 and 1999 the number of households living in chronic long-term poverty fell, from 4 per cent of households to 2.5 per cent of households.

Poverty rates are higher amongst:

- women;
- children;
- adults living in one-person households, including single pensioners;
- large families;
- families with a child under 11;
- young people;
- those who left school at age 16 or under;
- households with no paid workers;
- separated/divorced households;
- lone parent households;
- local authority and housing association tenants;
- households dependent on Income Support.

The poverty rate was 66 per cent and 62 per cent respectively for lone parents with one or two children and even higher for lone parents with three or more children. It was 77 per cent for unemployed people, and 61 per cent for disabled or long-term sick people, in households where no one was in paid work.

Absolute and overall poverty

This report also uses subjective measures to estimate how many people consider themselves to be in 'absolute' and 'overall' poverty according to the United Nations definitions: the findings were 17 per cent and 26 per cent respectively. The amount respondents thought was necessary to escape from absolute poverty was on average £178 per week. The average needed to escape from overall poverty was £239. Over 40 per cent of lone parents, 19 per cent of single pensioners and 18 per cent of couples with one child identified themselves as being in 'absolute' poverty and more than 50 per cent, 26 per cent and 27 per cent, respectively, as being in 'overall' poverty.

This represents a first attempt to operationalise an internationally agreed definition that can compare poverty consistently across countries. A future report based on the PSE survey will aim to go further, and operationalise these definitions objectively as well as by asking people about their perceptions.

The implications of these results are substantial. For example, they have implications for the adequacy of current benefit rates and wages in allowing people to achieve a living standard that takes them out of absolute and overall poverty, an aim that the British Government has signed up to at the United Nations.

Social exclusion

The PSE survey distinguishes four dimensions of exclusion: impoverishment, or exclusion from adequate income or resources; labour market exclusion; service exclusion; and exclusion from social relations. In this report our analysis has concentrated on the three dimensions that are distinct from poverty itself, with particular emphasis on exclusion from social relations.

Labour market exclusion
We should be cautious about treating non-participation in paid work or living in a jobless household as constituting social exclusion because:

- 43 per cent of adults have no paid work;

- over 1 in 3 of the population lives in a household without paid work: in which all adults are either pensioners or jobless non-pensioners.

However, labour market exclusion remains an important risk factor for both service exclusion and some aspects of exclusion from social relations.

Service exclusion

- More than 1 in 20 have been disconnected from water, gas, electricity or telephone and over 1 in 10 have used less than they need because of cost.

- About 1 in 14 are excluded from four or more of a list of essential public and private services and nearly 1 in 4 from two or more because the services are either unaffordable or unavailable.

- Non-availability of services (collective exclusion) is a bigger barrier than non-affordability (individual exclusion).

- Only about half the population has access to the full range of services.

Exclusion from social relations

- Of a list of common social activities, 1 in 10 people in the survey is excluded by cost from five or more activities and 1 in 5 from three or more.

- Lack of time due to caring responsibilities, paid work and disability also excludes people from socially necessary activities.

- One in 8 people has neither a family member nor a friend outside their household with whom they are in contact on a daily basis.

- Economic inactivity and living in a jobless household do not necessarily increase social isolation. In some cases, they reduce it.

- Men living alone have a high risk of social isolation.

- Nearly 11 per cent of the population have very poor personal support available in times of need (lack it in five or more of the seven situations listed in Table 30) and a further 12 per cent have poor support (lack it in four items).

- One in 10 of the population has no civic engagement at all.

Developing a scientific approach to poverty

During the twentieth century the scourge of infectious diseases was virtually eliminated in industrialised countries. A far more ambitious aim for the twenty-first century, an end to world poverty, will only be achieved if the political will and scientific expertise becomes available to develop and implement effective and efficient anti-poverty policies. Poverty and social exclusion are not Acts of God, nor are they an inevitable consequence of economic and social progress.

Scientific surveys like the Poverty and Social Exclusion Survey of Britain are necessary to provide details on the extent and nature of the problem. Without detailed knowledge it is impossible to develop effective policies. In 1998, the British Government committed itself to publishing an annual assessment of progress in reducing poverty and social exclusion. The first of these reports was published in late 1999 (DSS, 1999b). Three sets of indicators covering children and young people, people of working age, and older people were nominated to be used by the Government to monitor the success of their anti-poverty strategies. But there was no systematic measure of poverty like the ones in this survey. These types of data have not been included in any of the routine government-sponsored national surveys.[2]

In past years techniques pioneered by academic researchers have been picked up and incorporated into the routine surveys of the Office for National Statistics. If the Government, with independent scientific involvement of its own statisticians in the work, is going to be able to monitor its achievements in reducing poverty and social exclusion, it is to be hoped that the same will happen in this case.

The future

There is no doubt that lack of paid work is an important factor in causing both poverty and social exclusion. However, even if full employment were achieved, poverty and exclusion would not disappear. Earnings can be too low unless child benefit and other dependency allowances complement them. People who cannot work require adequate incomes to meet their needs. High quality, affordable services in every part of the country will also be needed if poverty and social exclusion are to be eliminated.

Britain has become an increasingly polarised nation, containing stark social and economic divisions. The growth of poverty is the root cause of many of the social ills that are of public concern. There is considerable unease in British society about the consequences of deprivation and the lack of social justice that this implies. If Britain is to become an inclusive society in which everybody has a stake and is able to participate then the most important task facing the Government is the ending of poverty and social exclusion.

Britain is at a crossroads of social development in terms of adopting effective measures to stop and then reverse the damaging structural trend which has increased poverty. During the 1980s incomes substantially diverged and in the late 1990s were continuing to diverge. The growth in poverty is the most critical social problem that Britain now faces. Problems of dislocation, insecurity, multiple deprivation, conflict, divided loyalties and divided activities all result. Major questions are being posed for the future of social cohesion. High rates of poverty and social exclusion have the effects of worsening health, education, skills in the changing labour market, relationships within the family, between ethnic groups and in society generally. The structural problem has to be addressed in a concerted national strategy. The construction of a scientific consensus - to improve measurement, explain severity and cause so that the right policies are selected, and show how the role of public and private services can be extended to underpin national life - is a key step in achieving the objectives set by the Government.

Notes

1   Also see ONS, 1997; and Scottish Homes, 1997.

2   A partial exception involves some elements included in the British Household Panel Survey. The measures of poverty summarised in this report are a measure of deprivation, a socially supported measure of necessities, and a measure of poverty, together with objective and subjective measures of 'absolute' and 'overall' poverty, the two-level approach to the measure of poverty agreed at Copenhagen in 1995. The approach to the measurement of social exclusion now recommended, that is labour market exclusion, service exclusion, exclusion from social relations, together with impoverishment or exclusion from financial resources, will allow the effects of different institutional changes and policies affecting trends to be monitored and assessed.

Appendix 1: Measures of poverty

Approach	Description	Advantages	Disadvantages	Used in the PSE survey
Consensual/ social indicators	Townsend first pioneered the use of social indicators in his scale of relative deprivation for his mammoth study of *Poverty in the United Kingdom* (1979). The techniques were developed further in the Breadline Britain surveys of 1983 and 1990 (Mack and Lansley, 1985; Gordon and Pantazis, 1997). The construction and use of a deprivation index was also developed in a Greater London survey in the late 1980s (Townsend and Gordon, 1989). Mack and Lansley's consensual approach has had a big impact on modern poverty research. Their original 1983 study was replicated in Britain in 1990 (Gordon and Pantazis, 1997) and in Wales in 1995 (Gordon, 1995). Local authorities in London, Manchester, Liverpool and Kent have conducted similar surveys. The Office of Population, Censuses and Surveys (OPCS) used a similar set of questions to measure the standard of living of disabled adults and families with disabled children in Britain in 1985 (Martin and White, 1988; Smyth and Robus, 1989; Gordon et al., 2000). Similarly, representative surveys were carried out by the PPRU amongst disabled people in Northern Ireland in 1990 and 1991 (Zarb and Maher, 1997). The European Statistical Office (Eurostat) has used a similar set of questions to measure standard of living in Britain and the 14 other member states annually since 1994 as part of the European Community Household Panel Survey (Ramprakash, 1994; Vogel, 1997; Eurostat, 1999). This approach to measuring the standard of living has also been adopted in Denmark (Mack and Lansley, 1985), Sweden (Halleröd, 1994, 1995a, 1995b, 1998), Ireland (Callan, Nolan and Whelan, 1993; Nolan and Whelan, 1996a), Belgium (Van den Bosch, 1998), Holland (Muffels et al., 1990; Muffels and Vries, 1991; Muffels, Berghman and Dirven, 1992), Finland (Kangas and Ritakillio, 1998), Germany (Andreß and Lipsmeir, 1995) and Vietnam (Davies and Smith, 1998).	Socially perceived necessities are chosen democratically on the basis of (a) identifying goods and activities common in society, and (b) inviting the public to identify those they regard as necessary – through this 'consensual' method.	The method is as yet not used routinely in government surveys. The list of items and activities is chosen by the researcher, albeit based on preliminary research - this is not an important criticism given the high reliablity of the measurement of deprivation.	Yes, extensively.

Approach	Description	Advantages	Disadvantages	Used in the PSE survey
Social exclusion	Social exclusion is the lack or denial of access to the kinds of social relations, social customs and activities in which the great majority of people in British society engage. In current usage, exclusion is often regarded as a 'process' rather than a 'state' and this helps in being constructively precise in deciding its relationship to poverty (among the key texts consulted are Levitas, 1999; Silver, 1994, pp. 531-78; Gore and Figueiredo, 1996; Room, 1995).	It has the potential of establishing a multi-dimensional measure conceptually independent of poverty measures.	This is the first attempt to operationalise social exclusion empirically, using primary survey data.	In this survey we have sought to collect data relevant to the concept of social exclusion.
Subjective measures	This approach to identifying poverty thresholds is also known as the income proxy method (Veit-Wilson, 1987), consensual poverty lines (see Walker, 1987, Halleröd, 1995a, for discussion) or Sociovital Minimum Income Level (SMIL) (Callan et al., 1989). Subjective poverty lines are estimations by populations (obtained through surveys) about the minimum income level at which people find it is still possible to live 'decently'. In most cases, the subjective method produces poverty lines at a relatively higher level of income than some expect. Deleeck et al. (1992) have argued that, in many cases, the poverty line is at such a level that it would be very difficult to maintain that all households below it are poor, in the sense of being socially excluded. They suggest that the term 'insecurity of subsistence', meaning a situation in which households encounter some (financial) difficulty in participating in the average or most widely shared lifestyle, would be more appropriate. All methods of estimating a subjective poverty line make use of a Minimum Income Question (MIQ) designed to measure the smallest income required to avoid 'poverty', live 'decently' or 'adequately' or to 'get along'. However, the exact wording of the MIQ varies considerably in different studies (Bradbury, 1989; Callan and Nolan, 1991). The simplest and arguably most democratic method of producing a 'subjective' poverty line is to use the average response to the Minimum Income Question from the population (survey sample) as a whole. This is a procedure that has been used in Britain (Townsend and Gordon, 1991; Townsend et al., 1996, 1997) and Australia (Saunders and Matheson, 1992). However, several other methods have been used in European countries (see Goedhart et al., 1977; Van Praag et al., 1980; Deleeck et al., 1988).	The most important advantage of the subjective method is that the level of the poverty line is not fixed by experts, but defined by society itself. The subjective method is therefore a socially realistic method.	Empirical studies have shown that estimates of the subjective poverty line usually rise systematically with the actual income of the household/-individual (Citro and Michael, 1995). Therefore, subjective poverty lines tend to fluctuate over time depending on changes in the social reference group (e.g. due to an increase in the overall living standard of elderly people, they respond with a higher necessary minimum income) and on the period of reference (e.g. in a period of crisis aspirations might decline).	In this survey we have used this technique in operationalising the UN standards of absolute and overall poverty. Similarly, subjectively perceived poverty lines have been measured in the PSE survey by asking respondents if their income is 'a lot below' the income needed to avoid poverty and 'a lot below' the income needed to avoid 'absolute' and 'overall' poverty. Respondents were also asked if they considered themselves to be 'genuinely poor now - all the time'.

Approach	Description	Advantages	Disadvantages	Used in the PSE survey
Income thresholds	Defining poverty purely in terms of low income is the most widely used method of measuring poverty. The poor are defined as those people/households with an income (or, more rarely, expenditure) below a certain threshold level irrespective of their standard of living. There were three approaches. One was (a) the income provided by the state in its payment of benefit. Thus in their seminal study, *The poor and the poorest*, Abel-Smith and Townsend (1965) adopted an income threshold related to the then National Assistance scales and later this kind of conventional or 'state' standard was adopted for many years by government in the Low Income Statistics series. This approach was abandoned by the Conservative Government in favour of a more out and out relative income standard in the Households Below Average Income (HBAI) series, which represented a second approach (b) relating income to a proportion of the average (usually 50 per cent of the mean in the UK but 60 per cent of the median in Europe). The third approach is (c) to find objectively the level of income correlating with multiple and material and social deprivation.	(a) The standard of need is implicit in the benefit levels decided by government. (b) The main advantage is its simplicity, as detailed information on the living conditions of the population is not required. (c) The threshold that is chosen depends on externally investigated levels of material and social deprivation.	(a) The problem with using benefit levels as income thresholds is that when they are increased in real terms so are the numbers defined as poor. (b) The problem with the thresholds based on average or median income is that they are essentially arbitrary cut-off points on the income distribution – really measure of inequality. Most economic poverty indices are really measures of income inequality rather than poverty (Townsend, 1979). Income is a poor indicator of command over resources over time. Economic poverty lines define the 'poor' as those with a low income even if they have a high standard of living. (c) There are problems in measuring the entire range of material and social needs, as well as resources that augment income.	Income thresholds have been used to measure poverty in this research.

Approach	Description	Advantages	Disadvantages	Used in the PSE survey
Budget standards	In the pre-war period poverty was studied using, as an income threshold, a budget standard, based on a basket of goods (mainly food) representing minimum subsistence/basic needs/absolute standards. This was the approach adopted by Rowntree in his three studies of poverty in York (1901, 1941, 1951) and by Beveridge (1942) in setting the original scales of social assistance. Budget standards involve drawing up a list of commodities, employing normative judgements, supported by a combination of scientific and behavioural evidence. The budget is then priced and used as an income standard – anyone living below that standard is in poverty. In Britain budget standards have been derived to represent a minimum adequate standard and a modest but adequate standard (Bradshaw, 1993). The US poverty standard was originally based on a budget standard (Orshansky, 1965).	The main advantage is that a budget standard is transparent. Items can easily be put into or taken out of a budget standard.	Budget standards are very labour intensive to establish and involve a host of normative judgements about the contents of the basket. They are also difficult to keep up to date. A basket of goods and services does not encompass all elements that make a standard of living. The pre-war budget standards assumed that there were basic or absolute needs regardless of the time and place.	Budget standards based poverty measures have not been used in this research as a measure of poverty, but were used to establish the PSE equivalence scale.

Appendix 2: Defining the objective scientific poverty line

Theory

From the discussion in Chapter 2, it is clear that people/households with a low income and a low standard of living are poor whereas those with a high income and a high standard of living are not poor. However, two other groups of people/households that are 'not poor' can also be identified in a cross-sectional (one point in time) survey, such as the Poverty and Social Exclusion Survey of Britain:

- *People/households with a low income but a high standard of living (the 'vulnerable').* This group is not currently poor but, if their income remains low, they will become poor - they are currently vulnerable to poverty. This situation often arises when income falls rapidly (e.g. due to job loss) but people manage to maintain their lifestyle, for at least a few months, by drawing on their savings and using the assets accumulated when income was higher.

- *People/households with a high income but a low standard of living (the 'risen').* This group is currently 'not poor' and if their income remains high their standard of living will rise – they have risen out of poverty. This group is in the opposite situation to the previous group. This situation can arise when the income of someone who is poor suddenly increases (e.g. due to getting a job); however, it takes time before people are able to buy the things that they need to increase their standard of living. Income can both rise and fall faster than standard of living.

A cross-sectional 'poverty' survey can provide some limited but useful information on the dynamics of poverty since it is possible not only to identify the 'poor' and the 'not poor' but also those vulnerable to poverty (i.e. people/households with a low income but a high standard of living) and those who have escaped from poverty (i.e. people/households with a high income but a low standard of living).

Poverty is, by definition, an extremely unpleasant situation to live in so it is not surprising that people go to considerable lengths to avoid it and try very hard to escape from poverty once they have sunk into it. Therefore, any cross-sectional poverty survey ought to find that the group of households at risk of poverty (the vulnerable) was larger than the group escaping from poverty since, when income falls people will try to delay the descent into poverty but, if the income of a poor person increases, they will quickly try to improve their standard of living.

Figure A1 illustrates this concept.

Between Time 0 and 1, the household has both a high standard of living and a high income: it is 'not poor'. At Time 1, there is a rapid reduction in income (e.g. due to job loss, the end of seasonal contract income, divorce or separation, etc.). However, the household's standard of living does not fall immediately. It is not until Time 2 that the household's standard of living has also fallen below the 'poverty' threshold. Therefore, between Time 1 and Time 2, the household is 'not poor' but is sinking into poverty (i.e. it has a low income but a relatively high standard of living). At Time 3, income begins to rise rapidly, although not as fast as it previously fell. This is because rapid income increases usually result from gaining employment but there is often a lag between starting work and getting paid. Standard of living also begins to rise after a brief period as the household spends its way out of poverty. However, this lag means that there is a short period when the household has a high

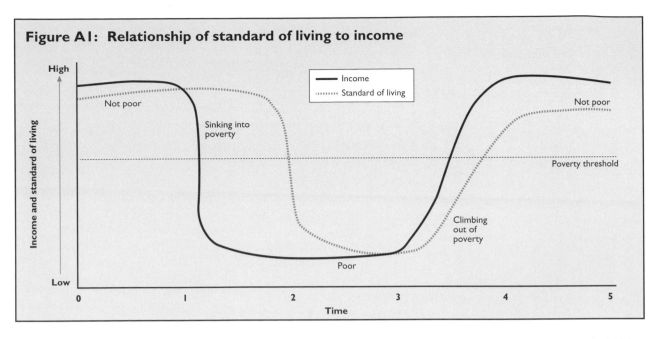

Figure A1: Relationship of standard of living to income

income but a relatively low standard of living. By Time 5, the household again has a high income and a high standard of living.

Measuring deprivation

In order to measure deprivation scientifically, it is necessary to construct a reliable, valid and additive deprivation index (Gordon and Townsend, 1990; Gordon, 1995). An initial deprivation index was constructed by summing the number of deprivation items that respondents said they 'did not have because they could not afford'. Only deprivation items were selected for the initial index that more than 50 per cent of the adults in the June 1999 ONS Omnibus Survey had considered to be necessities of life which all adults should be able to afford. The reliability of each item in the index was then tested using both classical reliability analysis models (Cronbach's alpha) and also Logistic Test Item Analysis (Nunnally, 1981). The validity of each item in the index was tested by calculating the correlation (Risk Ratio) between the item and two health variables (General Health Question and Limiting Long-Term Illness) and four perceptions of poverty variables (genuinely poor now 'all the time', income 'a lot below' the poverty line, income 'a lot below' the absolute and overall poverty line). These variables are robust measures of validity since there is now overwhelming evidence that poverty causes ill health (Independent Inquiry into Inequalities in Health, 1998; Davey Smith and

Gordon, 2000; Gordon et al., 1999; Shaw et al., 1999; Townsend and Davidson, 1988; Whitehead, 1988) and it would be expected at the population level that respondents who can objectively be defined as living in poverty would also be more likely to perceive themselves as poor compared with their non-poor peers.

Table A1 summarises the reliability and validity results. Overall, the 35 item index had a Cronbach's alpha of 0.8853 which is indicative of a highly reliable index. Nunnally has argued that:

in the early stages of research...one saves time and energy by working with instruments that have modest reliability, for which purpose reliabilities of 0.70 or higher will suffice...for basic research, it can be argued that increasing reliabilities much beyond 0.80 is often wasteful of time and funds, at that level correlations are attenuated very little by measurement error. (Nunnally, 1981)

The items that were not included in the index, as there was little evidence that they were either valid or reliable, were:

• television;
• refrigerator;
• beds and bedding for everyone;
• washing machine.

Table A1: Validity and reliability summary table

	Number of non significant validity indicators	Level of reliability (bold = unreliable)
Television	5	.8859
Medicines prescribed by doctor	4	.8851
Refrigerator	3	.8859
Beds and bedding for everyone	2	.8856
Washing machine	2	**.8854**
Telephone	2	.8845
Deep freezer/fridge freezer	2	.8848
Visits to friends or family	1	.8835
Visits to school, e.g. sports day	1	**.8858**
Collect children from school	1	**.8856**
Appropriate clothes for job interviews	1	.8814
Carpets in living rooms and bedrooms	1	.8824
Dictionary	1	.8843

Notes: Deprivation index Alpha = .8853

Additivity

The components of any deprivation index should be additive; e.g. a person or household with a deprivation score of three should be poorer than a person or household with a deprivation score of two (Gordon, 1995). It is necessary to check that all components of a deprivation index are additive. This was done by examining both the main effects and all possible second order interaction effects between the components of the deprivation index using equivalised income as the dependent variable. Income outliers had first been removed using standard robust Exploratory Data Analysis techniques (e.g. Boxplots). This resulted in all households with net incomes above £895 per week, which is the equivalent of an annual income after tax of over £46,500 per year and approximately £77,500 gross annual income, not being included in the final poverty threshold model. Examination of the second order interactions showed that not being able to afford 'all medicines prescribed by a doctor' was not additive with 18 other deprivation items. Similarly, not being able to afford 'a deep freezer/fridge freezer' was not additive with seven other derivation items, so both these items were not included in the final valid, reliable and additive deprivation index.

Finding the 'objective' poverty line

General Linear Models (both ANOVA and logistic regression) were used to determine the scientific poverty threshold, e.g. the deprivation score that maximises the between-group differences and minimises the within-group differences (sum of squares). These techniques were applied to a succession of groups created by increasing the number of items that respondents did not have because they could not afford them. Thus, the first analysis was undertaken on groups defined by households lacking no items compared with households lacking one or more items (a deprivation score of one or more). Similarly, the second analysis was undertaken on a group comprised of households lacking one or no items against two or more items, and so forth.

The dependent variable in the ANOVA model was net household income and the independent variables were deprivation group (constructed as described above), number of adults in each household and the number of children in each household. With the logistic regression models, the dependent variable was the deprivation group and

Table A2: Brief summary table for ANOVA and logistic regression models of optimum position for the poverty threshold

Model	F Statistic for corrected ANOVA Model	logistic regression model Chi-square
Null Model	26	
Deprivation score of 1 or more	45	145
Deprivation score of 2 or more	51	223
Deprivation score of 3 or more	45	205
Deprivation score of 4 or more	42	192
Deprivation score of 5 or more	36	170
Deprivation score of 6 or more	31	126

the independent variables were net household income, number of adults and number of children. Both the ANOVA and logistic regression models yielded the same final result – that a score of two or more on the deprivation index was the optimum position for the poverty line. Summary results are shown in Table A2.

Identifying the rising and the vulnerable groups

In a cross-sectional survey there will probably be a few people who have recently 'risen out of poverty', e.g. those with a high deprivation score and a high income. Their incomes and/or 'standard of living' should have increased in the recent past. These few cases were identified using boxplots of income by 'multiply deprived' group (i.e. with a deprivation score of 2 or more) and controlling for household size/type. The outliers (with high incomes) in each household type should be those risen out of poverty.

There should also be a much larger group of households who have relatively low incomes but are not yet suffering from multiple deprivation (i.e. the vulnerable to poverty group who have incomes equivalent to the median incomes of the multiply deprived – two or more group). Thus, using these definitions, the Poverty and Social Exclusion Survey of Britain found that, at the end of the last millennium:

* 25.6 per cent of people were living in poverty;

* 1.8 per cent had risen out of poverty;

* 10.3 per cent were potentially vulnerable to poverty;

* almost two-thirds (62.2 per cent) were relatively well off.

Appendix 3: Creation of the child deprivation index

Introduction

A child deprivation index was constructed following the general procedures set out above. Briefly, items that over half of parents believed to be necessary were retained for consideration in the index. This resulted in 27 of the 30 items being retained (see Chapter 4, Table 14). Validity tests were made on each item whereby the odds of a child lacking the item because their parent(s) could not afford it were checked against the four subjective measures of poverty described above. All valid items were then assessed to establish if they were measuring the same single dimension of deprivation. Finally,[1] an exploration was undertaken to establish the appropriate number of items of which a child had to be deprived to classify the child as poor.

Two population bases were possible for this analysis: first, households with children; second, the total number of children. Though either base is legitimate, the latter was deemed to provide information of more direct relevance to the study.

Time constraints did not allow the deprivation items to be asked separately for each child in the questionnaire. Instead, the respondent was asked about deprivation for any child in the family. A number of the items are age-related, such as attending play-group, so any positive responses on these items for children of inappropriate ages were excluded from counting towards the scale (see Table A3).

Validating the items

Individual items with no significant association with other measures of poverty were to be excluded from further analysis. However, only two items were found to be independent of one of the subjective poverty measures: toys and own books (Table A4).

Table A3: Age adjusted items

	Age			
	Babies	Pre-school	Primary school	Secondary school
Toys (e.g. dolls, teddies)	+	+	+	-
Leisure equipment	-	-	+	+
Bedrooms for every child of different sex	-	-	+	+
Bike: new/second-hand	-	+	+	+
All required school uniform	-	-	+	+
Hobby or leisure activity	-	-	+	+
Play group (pre-school age children)	+	+	-	-
School trip at least once a term	-	-	+	+
Friends round for tea/snack	-	-	+	+

Note: + deprivation response allowed

  - deprivation response excluded

Table A4: The odds of being deprived of an item according to subjective poverty status

	Poor all the time	Poverty	Absolute poverty	Overall poverty
Three meals a day	4.69	2.34	3.02	24.79
Toys (e.g. dolls, teddies)*	3.65	**1.04**	--	--
Leisure equipment	3.04	4.30	4.83	4.86
Bedrooms for every child of different sex*	2.39	1.24	0.85	1.64
Warm, waterproof coat	2.94	6.67	7.27	6.30
Books of own	7.26	**1.01**	--	--
Bike: new/second-hand*	1.65	1.07	1.51	2.97
Construction toys	3.97	3.52	4.64	4.44
Educational games	7.72	5.24	9.10	5.24
New, properly fitted, shoes	1.68	6.89	9.07	6.04
At least 7 pairs of new underpants	4.60	12.33	13.03	10.63
At least 4 jumpers/cardigans/sweatshirts	4.73	4.79	8.58	5.31
All required school uniform*	2.63	5.44	10.10	7.06
At least 4 pairs of trousers	4.90	3.68	3.78	2.80
Meat, fish or vegetarian equivalent at least twice a day	5.23	8.78	9.95	6.91
Fresh fruit or vegetables daily	9.64	8.64	11.29	9.48
Garden to play in	2.00	3.27	4.04	9.85
New, not second-hand, clothes	3.06	7.26	7.61	4.66
Carpet in bedroom	6.18	5.54	4.39	3.73
Beds and bedding for everyone	7.53	4.71	6.08	4.01
Hobby or leisure activity*	7.20	5.16	9.37	9.03
Celebrations on special occasions	39.53	6.96	9.12	21.36
Swimming at least once a month	3.51	10.63	9.34	11.65
Play group (pre-school age children)*	**0.90**	2.99	1.58	6.03
Annual week's holiday	3.46	3.91	4.44	3.62
School trip at least once a term*	6.39	7.88	6.29	4.92
Friends round for tea/snack*	7.00	6.85	7.95	6.85
N	795	729	724	715
Proportion poor	0.12	0.21	0.18	0.34

Notes: – cannot be computed: one of cells is zero in the 4 way table.

Figures in bold typeface are not significant at P<0.05 and therefore do not contribute to the overall reliability of the index.

* age-adjusted items

The overall number of significance tests used could easily have resulted in these two items being significant (at P<0.05) by chance. In contrast, both of these necessities showed a positive association with the respondent's perception that they were poor all the time. All children deprived of these two necessities were also poor on the absolute and overall poverty measures – which is why the odds ratio could not be formed for these items. Thus, overall, the two necessities showed a positive association with three out of the four subjective measures and, hence, were accepted as valid indicators of poverty.

The reliability of the scale

Reliability can be measured in a number of ways. Table A5 shows the Cronbach's alpha analysis for the children's deprivation index. The items highlighted in bold do not contribute to the overall reliability of the index.

Table A5: Children's items reliability analysis

	Corrected item total correlation	Alpha if item removed
Three meals a day	0.3620	0.8297
Toys (e.g. dolls, teddies)*	0.2992	0.8318
Leisure equipment*	0.4528	0.8250
Bedrooms for every child of different sex*	**0.0865**	**0.8393**
Warm, waterproof coat	0.4013	0.8276
Books of own	0.2189	0.8337
Bike: new/second-hand*	0.2645	0.8325
Construction toys	0.4495	0.8253
Educational games	0.5580	0.8203
New, properly fitted, shoes	0.3614	0.8287
At least 7 pairs of new underpants	0.5151	0.8239
At least 4 jumpers/cardigans/sweatshirts	0.4973	0.8232
All required school uniform*	0.3441	0.8292
At least 4 pairs of trousers	0.4717	0.8242
Meat, fish or vegetarian equivalent at least twice a day	0.5366	0.8212
Fresh fruit or vegetables daily	0.4266	0.8268
Garden to play in	**0.1332**	**0.8373**
New, not second-hand, clothes	0.5393	0.8219
Carpet in bedroom	0.2543	0.8319
Beds and bedding for everyone	0.2411	0.8324
Hobby or leisure activity*	0.4461	0.8254
Celebrations on special occasions	0.4227	0.8272
Swimming at least once a month	0.4535	0.8249
Play group (pre-school age children)*	0.1571	0.8339
Annual week's holiday	**0.3340**	**0.8396**
School trip at least once a term*	0.3859	0.8284
Friends round for tea/snack*	0.4625	0.8246

Notes: Overall alpha 0.8339

Items highlighted in bold do not contribute to the overall reliability of the index

* age-adjusted items

The exclusion of three items (separate bedrooms for opposite sex siblings aged over 10, a garden to play in, a holiday away from home) would have improved the alpha level by a small extent. However, as the gain was minimal, it was decided to retain these items for the purposes of the present investigation, although further sensitivity tests are planned to investigate the consequences of excluding particular items.

Identifying a poverty threshold

Answering the question 'What is the appropriate number of items a child should be deprived of before being considered poor?' is not straightforward. The essential concept underlying the scale is that children lack necessities because their parents cannot afford to buy them. From this perspective, it is arguable that the parent's current income should be reflected in the child's deprivation score. However, there are many reasons why the two may not match. For example, a family whose income has recently dropped may be protected against poverty by drawing on savings or because a number of the necessities are linked to a life span that may outlast short periods of poverty (e.g. clothes and material goods).

Family income was chosen as a basis for comparing the similarity of children classified as poor and not poor on the deprivation scale. A sequential approach was adopted whereby children first were classified as poor if they lacked one or more necessities and not poor otherwise. This was then extended to two or more items as poor, and so forth. The extent to which poor children were more similar to each other whereas non-poor children were more similar to each other - subsequently maximising differences between the two groups - was undertaken using discriminant function analysis (DFA).

DFA predicts group membership (poor versus non-poor) according to a set of explanatory variables indexing children's characteristics. Income is the main criterion by which the two groups are separated, however, controls are also required for family composition. DFA works by assessing the between-group differences relative to within group differences, which is equivalent to minimising within-group differences. A number of statistics are produced including the eigenvalue (the between-group sum of squares relative to the within-group sum of squares) relating to the discriminatory function. It is the eigenvalue that enables us to assess the extent to which within-group similarities and between-group differences vary as the poverty line is changed from one or more items to two or more items, and so forth. The results of three sets of analyses are reported varying the minimum number of necessities lacking from one to three. Two models were used for each analysis: the first focused solely on family composition, the second included both family composition and income.

Prior to considering the results, a word of caution is in order. The income variable available was gross of any housing costs. In other words, it was not possible to assess how much income was available to the family after housing costs were accounted for. This is problematic because two families with the same income could have very different housing costs and thus one group would have less to spend on themselves and their children after paying the mortgage or rent. Therefore, not all people on high income will necessarily have larger amounts of money potentially available for the children and, similarly, people on lower incomes with moderate housing costs may actually have relatively large proportions of their gross income available.

The results of the analysis suggested that the appropriate distinction was between no necessities and one or more necessities: the eigenvalue was greatest for the two models applied to this distinction. Further, the additional increase in the eigenvalue comparing the two models was also highest for this distinction, which shows the impact of income, rather than family composition, in discriminating between the two groups.

Table A6: Eigenvalues associated with predicting deprivation on the basis of family composition and income including all items in the scale

Number of items making up the deprivation group	Model 1	Model 2
One or more	.082	.182
Two or more	.070	.114
Three or more	.066	.114

Note: Model 1 includes the number of adults and the number of children in the family, both measured with three levels, as one, two and three or more. Model 2 adds net household income, transformed to a natural log scale, to Model 1.

Summary

A scale measuring childhood poverty using 27 necessities was produced. The validity of the items partly lies in the fact that they were devised by parents from differing background but also because each item is significantly associated with other measures of poverty. In general, the items form an internally consistent measure of poverty. Using the DFA results suggests a cut-off of one or more necessities as the classification for poverty. However, concerns with the income variable suggest caution over accepting these initial results.

Note

1   It was not possible to evaluate the additivity of the items, as described for adults, due to the much smaller sample of households with children.

Appendix 4: The 1999 Poverty and Social Exclusion Survey of Britain: Technical report

Introduction

The Poverty and Social Exclusion Survey of Britain was carried out by the Social Survey Division of the Office for National Statistics and was supported by the Joseph Rowntree Foundation. This appendix describes the survey design, sampling, data collection and fieldwork procedures and the processing of the survey. It also includes a comparison of responding and non-responding households.

Background and aims

The Poverty and Social Exclusion Survey of Britain (PSE) was designed to update the Breadline Britain surveys which were conducted by MORI in 1983 and 1990 (Gordon and Pantazis, 1997) and to improve the methodology, particularly by the use of probability sampling. There were two parts to the PSE survey. First, a representative sample of the population of Great Britain was asked for their views on what constitute the necessities of life in present-day Britain.

The June 1999 Omnibus Survey

The 'necessities of life' questions were asked in the June 1999 Office for National Statistics Omnibus Survey. Respondents were interviewed in their own homes and given sets of shuffled cards and asked:

"On these cards are a number of different items which relate to our standard of living. I would like you to indicate the living standards you feel all adults should have in Britain today by placing the cards in the appropriate box. BOX A is for items which you think are necessary; which all adults should be able to afford and which

they should not have to do without. BOX B is for items which may be desirable but are not necessary."

A similar question was asked with regard to necessities for children. Full details can be found on the web at URL, http://qb.soc.surrey.ac.uk/surveys/pses/psesintro.htm

A sample of 3,000 addresses was selected from the Postcode Address File of 'small users'. The sample from 100 postal sectors was stratified by:

- region;

- proportion of households renting from local authorities;

- proportion of households with heads in the professional, employer or manager socio-economic groups (SEG 1-5 & 13).

The 100 postal sectors were selected with probability proportionate to size, and within each sector 30 addresses were selected at random. If an address contained more than one household, the interviewer used the standard ONS procedure to randomly select just one household. Within each household, with more than one adult member, just one person aged 16 or over was selected using random number tables. All interviews were carried out face-to-face with the selected respondent and no proxy interviews were allowed.

The response rate was 69 per cent as shown in Table A7.

Table A7: June 1999 Omnibus Survey response rate

	Number	(%)
Selected addresses	3,000	100
Ineligible addresses	323	11
Eligible addresses	2,677	89
Refusals	588	22
Non-contact	234	9
Interviews achieved	**1,855**	**69**

The follow-up to the General Household Survey

A random follow-up sample was drawn from respondents to the 1998/9 General Household Survey, and interviewed in detail about their circumstances and their views on a range of issues associated with poverty and social exclusion.

The aims of the survey were:

- to update the Breadline Britain surveys;

- to estimate the size of groups of households in different circumstances;

- to explore movement in and out of poverty;

- to look at age and gender differences in experiences of and responses to poverty.

Although the survey is primarily concerned with the experience of people living in Britain, it is planned that similar surveys will also be carried out in other countries, using a questionnaire based on that developed for the PSE.

The survey design

The PSE survey was designed as a follow-up survey of respondents to the 1998/9 General Household Survey (GHS). This design made it possible to select a sample with known characteristics. It also meant that one person in each selected household could be sampled prior to fieldwork. Information from the original survey allowed the characteristics of PSE non-responders to be identified, allowing analysis of the effects of non-response bias.

Sample design

The sample design was influenced by three main considerations:

- sufficient cases were required for the analysis of key variables by sub-groups;

- sufficient cases were required for separate analysis of households and individuals in Scotland;

- sufficient cases of low-income households and respondents were required to examine their characteristics.

The sample design therefore gave a greater probability of selection to people in lower income groups and Scotland. Households in the lower income groups were identified by using a measure of equivalised income; that is, a measure of household income which takes account of household size and composition.

Selecting households from lower income groups: equivalised income measure

An equivalised income measure was developed by Jonathan Bradshaw and Sue Middleton in conjunction with the Office for National Statistics (ONS). The McClements equivalence scale, which is used as the standard by ONS (Government Statistical Service, 1998), was felt not to be appropriate for the PSE, as it does not assign sufficient weight to children, particularly young children. The scale used for the PSE was designed to take account of this. Each member of the household was assigned a value, shown in Table A8:

Table A8: Equivalised income scale

Type of household member	Equivalence value
Head of household	0.70
Partner	0.30
Each additional adult (anyone over 16)	0.45
Add for first child	0.35
Add for each additional child	0.30
If head of household is a lone parent, add	0.10

The values for each household member were added together to give the total equivalence value for that household. This number was then divided into the gross income for that household. For example, the equivalence value for a lone-parent household with two children is 0.7 + 0.35 + 0.3 + 0.1 = 1.45. If the household's gross income is £10,000, its equivalised income is £6,897 (= £10,000/1.45).

Equivalised income was grouped into quintiles, with the bottom quintile comprising households with the lowest incomes and the top quintile those households with the highest incomes. The quintiles were then sampled in the following proportions, as set out in Table A9:

Table A9: Probability of selection for income quintiles

Quintile group	Proportion sampled
Bottom quintile (lowest income)	40%
Fourth quintile	30%
Third quintile	10%
Second quintile	10%
Top quintile (highest income)	10%

Selecting areas, households and individuals for interview

Identifying individuals for interview involved a three-stage process. First, a number of areas were selected from all of those used for the 1998/9 GHS.

Second, a number of households were selected from each of the areas; third, one individual was chosen from each sampled household. To allow for variation in income within areas the list of primary sampling units (PSUs) was sorted on area and quintile group before any selections were made.

Areas

The 1998/9 GHS sample was selected from 576 PSUs based on postcode sectors. In order to ensure sufficient representation of the population in the PSE sample, 70 per cent of GHS areas in England and Wales were selected (360 areas from a total of 518[1]). All of the 54 Scottish areas were sampled to provide sufficient cases for separate analysis of the Scottish data.

Table A10: Number of areas sampled for the PSE

Area	GHS 1998 N	PSE 1999 N
England and Wales	518	360
Scotland	54	54
Total	576	414

Households

A sample of households was taken from each selected area.

Individuals

One adult aged 16 or over was selected at random from each sampled household, using a Kish grid. This was done in preference to interviewing all eligible adults because individuals in households tend to be similar to one another. Where households differ markedly from one another, the resultant clustering can lead to a substantial increase in the standard error around survey estimates. This is particularly true when asking opinion questions where household members may influence each other's answers. Only those who had given a full interview in 1998/9 were eligible for selection. Partial interviews and proxies were excluded from the eligible sample. In keeping with the aim of ensuring that sufficient interviews were carried out for analysis purposes, some reserves were selected, to be used if necessary.

If the selected adult was no longer resident in the household, interviewers were instructed not to substitute another household member for the sampled person, as that would adversely affect the representativeness of the sample. When the selected adult had moved house since the GHS interview, interviewers traced them to their new address if it was nearby and asked for an interview. Otherwise, the respondent was coded as having moved. In those households where the sampled individual agreed to the follow-up interview, interviewers updated the household composition, recording members who had moved out or died, and adding new members who had been born or moved into the household since the GHS interview. Table A11 shows changes in household composition in responding households.

Table A11: Changes to household composition of PSE responders

Changes to household composition	Number	(%)
Still in household	3329	95.7
Moved out (including deceased)	58	1.7
New to household (including births since GHS)	82	2.4
Missing	8	0.2
Total (all household members)	3477	100.0

Questionnaire content

As one of the aims of the PSE was to update the Breadline Britain surveys, questions which had been used in the previous surveys were repeated where possible, to maintain continuity and allow comparisons over time. The PSE survey did, however, aim to measure a variety of concepts of poverty and social exclusion and this involved some

redesign of the questionnaire and the development of new questions.

For example, new questions were included to measure respondent's assessments of absolute and overall poverty, as defined at the United Nations World Summit on Social Development in Copenhagen in 1995. The survey also tried to measure intra-household poverty.

The main topics covered in the questionnaire were:

- housing (including the condition of accommodation and satisfaction with accommodation);
- health (including disability, isolation and depression);
- time (time poverty);
- social networks and support;
- necessities (these questions were conducted as a card sorting exercise);
- finance and debts;
- intra-household poverty;
- poverty over time;
- absolute and overall poverty;
- area deprivation;
- local services;
- crime;
- child's school;
- perceptions of poverty;
- activism.

Choosing a survey design based on a follow-up of the GHS meant that detailed information was already available on those topics covered by the GHS interview, and questions did not have to be included in the PSE. As the follow-up interviews took place between six and 18 months after the original interview, a small number of follow-up questions was included in the PSE questionnaire to record changes to the household composition, employment and income.

Ten PSE interviewers each wrote a short report on how the questionnaire worked in the field. They reported that respondents found the subject matter of the survey interesting. Those who agreed to take part were enthusiastic and hopeful that the results of the survey would be put to good use. Some respondents used the questionnaire as an opportunity to air their problems (such as loneliness or problems with their local area).

The sections that the respondents found most difficult to answer were those on absolute and overall poverty, social networks and support, local services and the necessities questions which involved the card-sorting exercise. For some sections of the questionnaire, problems arose because respondents were being asked to think about things they would normally take for granted, such as the goods or services they owned or had access to. For other sections, respondents were being asked to think about things they would not usually consider, such as how much money they would need to keep their household out of poverty, and some found this very difficult to do.

Interviewers reported that respondents found the questions on local services repetitive and became bored and irritated. The crime section made some elderly respondents feel uneasy.

Data collection and fieldwork procedures

Advance letters

Advance letters were sent to sampled individuals, reminding them of their participation in the GHS, explaining the purpose of the PSE and asking for their co-operation with the follow-up interview. As a named respondent had been selected before the interview, the advance letter was addressed to the selected respondent by name. Where a name had not been provided by the respondent during the GHS interview, the advance letter was addressed to 'the resident'.

Contacting the respondent

Where contact telephone numbers were available, interviewers made initial contact with the respondent by telephone. This method of contacting respondents was used to reduce costs. Once an appointment was made with the respondent, the interviews were conducted face-to-face. In the event of a broken appointment, interviewers were

instructed to make a maximum of two visits at an address before recording a non-contact, unless they were already in the area and could make an extra call without driving out of their way.

Respondents who had moved house since taking part in the GHS were traced by interviewers if they had moved within the same area. Interviewers requested authorisation from their office-based supervisor before tracing respondents who had moved.

Data collection

Fieldwork took place between 1 September and 15 Ocober 1999. There were three types of data collection: face-to-face interviews, a self-completion module and a card-sorting exercise.

Face-to-face interviews were conducted using Computer-Assisted Personal Interviewing (CAPI). Interviewers recorded respondents' answers on laptop computers which had been programmed using Blaise software. Where applicable, a limited amount of proxy information was collected about the respondent's partner and child.

A Computer-Assisted Self-Interviewing (CASI) module was used to collect answers to sensitive questions, such as those on crime and for some questions on self-reported health. Where the respondent was reluctant or unable to complete the self-completion section on the lap-top the interviewer asked the respondent's permission to ask these questions.

As mentioned in the introduction, a representative sample of the population took part in the first part of the Poverty and Social Exclusion Survey of Britain in July 1999, carried out on the ONS Omnibus Survey. Respondents to that part of the survey were given a set of cards, on which were listed a number of items (one item per card), and were asked to say which of the items they considered were necessities in present-day Britain. Respondents to the GHS follow-up were asked to carry out a similar card-sorting exercise. In this case, the respondent was asked to place each card in a pile depending on whether they had the item; did not have it and could not afford it; or did not have the item and did not want it. Where problems with literacy or manual dexterity prevented the respondent from completing this exercise, the interviewer was permitted to read the cards and place them in the correct pile according to the respondent's answer.

Length of interview

The average length of interview was 60 minutes. With older respondents or those who had literacy problems, it took about 90 minutes. Questions requiring a lot of thought or those involving difficult concepts, such as assessments of absolute and overall poverty, were particularly taxing for some elderly respondents, a number of whom became quite tired during the interview.

The length of the questionnaire affected the response rate. ONS interviewers are required to give an assessment of how long the interview is likely to take when making an appointment, to ensure that respondents set aside sufficient time. Some sampled individuals refused to take part on hearing that the interview was likely to last for an hour. Because of

the relatively short field period (a month), interviewers also did not have sufficient time to call back on many households to attempt to persuade them to change their decision not to take part.

Response

Table A12 shows the response to the PSE follow-up interview. Of the 2,846 individuals selected, 415 (15 per cent) were ineligible because the sampled individual had moved or died, because the household could not be traced so it was not known whether the whole household had moved or because it was a reserve which was not issued to an interviewer.

Of the 2,431 eligible individuals, 1,534 (63 per cent) were interviewed, the vast majority completing a full interview. This response rate is disappointing and may reflect some of the factors outlined above. However, the availability of information about non-responders means that it is possible to compensate for non-response by weighting.

Table A12: Response to the PSE follow-up survey

Response category	Number of cases	Percentage of set sample	Percentage of eligible sample
Set sample	2846		
Ineligible			
Household not traced, reserve not issued	210	7.4	
Selected adult no longer resident	83	2.9	
Selected adult deceased	19	0.7	
Other ineligible	103	3.6	
Total ineligible	**415**	**14.6**	
Total eligible sample	2431	85.4	
Full interview	1530		62.9
Partial interview	4		0.2
Total co-operating	**1534**		**63.1**
Non-contact	180		7.4
Refusals			
Refusal to HQ	85		3.5
Refusal by household	113		4.6
Refusal by selected individual	470		19.3
Incapable of taking part	49		2.0
Total refusals	**717**		**29.5**

Where a refusal to the survey was given, the interviewer recorded the main reason given, which is shown in Table A13. The most common reasons for refusal were 'Can't be bothered' (20 per cent), 'Genuinely too busy' (14 per cent) and 'Too old or infirm' (12 per cent).

Table A13: Reasons for refusal (first reason given)

Reason for refusal	(%)
Can't be bothered	19.6
Genuinely too busy	14.2
Too old/infirm	12.3
Other reason	11.9
No reason given	9.8
Temporarily too busy	6.2
Broken appointments	6.0
Personal problems	5.5
Bad experience with previous surveys	4.2
Invasion of privacy	3.4
Late contact, insufficient time	2.1
About to go away	1.7
Doesn't believe in surveys	1.5
Disliked survey matter	0.6
Concerns about confidentiality	0.4
Refusal to HQ	0.2
Not capable	0.2
Base	583

Response to the self-completion section is shown in Table A14. Fifty-five per cent of respondents completed the section themselves on the laptop, while an additional 45 per cent were asked the questions by the interviewer. The level of self-completion is lower than is normal on surveys of this type. The Health Education Monitoring Survey (HEMS), for example, regularly asks respondents to key their answers in on the laptop and about 85 per cent of eligible respondents do so. The low proportion self-completing this section of the PSE may reflect the age profile of the PSE sample. Other surveys requiring self-completion often have an age cut-off; the HEMS only asks those aged 16 to 54 to self-complete. Problems with eyesight, which are more common among older people, are often cited

by those who decline to use the laptop. Willingness to self-complete could also have been affected by the position of the section at the end of the questionnaire, by which time respondents may have become fatigued. Evidence from interviewers suggests that this was the case, particularly for the elderly respondents.

Table A14: Response to the self-completion module

	Number	(%)
Respondent completed the section	844	55.0
Interviewer completed the section	683	44.5
Section refused or not completed	7	0.5
Base	1534	100

Weighting procedures

As noted earlier, the PSE interviewed one person per household, oversampled households in Scotland and oversampled households in the lowest quintile groups of equivalised income. Several weights were therefore calculated to allow for the probability of selection and also to compensate for non-response. Care must be taken to use the correct weight for the chosen analysis unit. Details of each of these elements and the weighting procedure are available from the authors (see Appendix 6).

Note

1 There were 522 GHS areas in England and Wales in 1998; 518 were used to select the PSE sample, as four had been used for the pilot study.

Appendix 5: List of Poverty and Social Exclusion Survey of Britain working Papers

1 Pantazis, C., Townsend, P. and Gordon, D. (2000) *The necessities of life in Britain*

2 Bradshaw, J., Middleton, S., Williams, J. and Ashworth, K. (2000) *The necessities of life for children*

3 Gordon, D., Pantazis, C. and Townsend, P. (2000) *Changing necessities of life 1983-99*

4 Gordon, D. (2000) *Income and social deprivation*

5 Townsend, P., Gordon, D. and Pantazis, C. (forthcoming UNRISD) *The international measurement of absolute and overall poverty*

6 Adelman, L., Ashworth, K. and Middleton, S. (2000) *Poverty, social exclusion and employment*

7 Ashworth, K., Middleton, S. and Adelman, L. (2000) *Social security, poverty and social exclusion*

8 Goodwin, D., Adelman, L. and Middleton, S. (2000) *Debt, money management and access to financial services*

9 Pantazis, C. and Middleton, S. (2000) *Poverty and gender*

10 Gordon, D. and Middleton, C. (2000) *Poverty and time*

11 Bradshaw, J. and Levitas, R. (2000) *Lone parent families, poverty and social exclusion*

12 Gordon, D. (2000) *Poverty and health/disablement*

13 Levitas, R., Pantazis, C. and Patsios, D. (2000) *Social exclusion as lack of social relations*

14 Bramley, G. (2000) *Social exclusion and lack of access to services*

15 Payne, S. (2000) *Poverty and mental health*

16 Pantazis, C. (2000) *Poverty and crime*

17 Bradshaw, J. (2000) *Active citizenship, social exclusion and social norms*

18 Bramley, G. (2000) *Social exclusion and local neighbourhoods*

19 Bradshaw, J. and Middleton, S. (2000) *Child poverty and social exclusion*

20 Patsios, D. (2000) *Poverty and social exclusion among the elderly*

21 Levitas, R., Bradshaw, J. and Townsend, P. (2000) *How multidimensional is social exclusion?*

22 Townsend, P., Levitas, R. and Gordon, D. (2000) *Establishing an operational definition of material and social deprivation, social exclusion and poverty*

23 Adelman, L., Ashworth, K. and Middleton, S. (2000) *Intra-household distribution of poverty and social exclusion*

24 Pantazis, C., Gordon, D. and Townsend, P. (2000)
    'Perceptions of the necessities of life: Scotland
    and England compared', Scottish Affairs
    Committee, *Poverty in Scotland*, Minutes of
    Evidence, House of Commons, HC59-V, London,
    TSO, pp123-27

25 Townsend, P. (2000) 'Prisoners of the global
    market: Social polarisation and poverty', in J.
    Baudot (ed.), *Building a world community:
    Globalisation and the common good*. A report of
    the Copenhagen Seminars, for the special session
    of the United Nations General Assembly on the
    follow-up to the Social Summit, Geneva 2000
    Forum, pp230-53

26 Townsend, P., Pantazis, C. and Gordon, D. (2000)
    'Perceptions of the necessities of life: Wales,
    England and Scotland compared', Select
    Committee on Welsh Affairs, *Inquiry into social
    exclusion*, London: The Stationery Office

Appendix 6: Contact details for the lead researchers

Professor Peter Townsend
Department of Social Policy
London School of Economics
Houghton Street
London WC2A 2AE
Email p.townsend@lse.ac.uk
Tel. 020 7955 6632
and
Townsend Centre for International Poverty Research
University of Bristol
8 Priory Road
Bristol BS8 1TZ
Tel. 0117 954 6771

Dr David Gordon
Townsend Centre for International Poverty Research
University of Bristol
8 Priory Road
Bristol BS8 1TZ
Email dave.gordon@bristol.ac.uk
Tel. 0117 954 6761
Fax 0117 954 6756

Dr Ruth Levitas
University of Bristol
12 Woodland Road
Bristol BS8 1UQ
Email ruth.levitas@bristol.ac.uk
Tel. 0117 928 7506
Fax 0117 970 6022

Sue Middleton
Centre for Research in Social Policy
Department of Social Sciences
Loughborough University
Loughborough LE11 3TU
Email s.middleton@lboro.ac.uk
Tel. 01509 223372
Fax 01509 213409

Professor Jonathan Bradshaw
Social Policy Research Unit
University of York
Heslington
York YO10 5DD
Email jrb1@york.ac.uk
Tel. 01904 433480
Fax 01904 433477

Glossary

BHPS	British Household Panel Survey
CAPI	Computer-Assisted Personal Interviewing
CASI	Computer-Assisted Self-Interviewing
CPAG	Child Poverty Action Group
CSO	Central Statistical Office
DSS	Department of Social Security (UK)
EEC	European Economic Community
Eurostat	European Statistical Office
FES	Family Expenditure Survey
FRS	Family Resources Survey
GHS	General Household Survey
GHQ	General Health Questionnaire
HBAI	Households Below Average Income
HEMS	Health Education Monitoring System
ILO	International Labour Organisation
MIQ	Minimum Income Question
MORI	Market and Opinion Research International
OECD	Organisation for Economic Co-operation and Development
ONS	Office for National Statistics
OPCS	Office of Population, Censuses and Surveys
PPRU	Policy Planning and Research Unit (Northern Ireland)
PSE	Poverty and Social Exclusion Survey
SD	Standard Deviation
SMIL	Sociovital Minimum Income Level
UN	United Nations
UNDP	United Nations Development Programme
UNICEF	United Nations Children's Fund
UNRISD	United Nations Research Institute for Social Development
WHO	World Health Organization

Bibliography

Abel-Smith, B. and Townsend, P. (1965) *The poor and the poorest: A new analysis of the Ministry of Labour's Family Expenditure Surveys of 1953-54 and 1960*, London: G. Bell & Sons

Andreß, H.J. (ed.) (1998) *Empirical poverty research in a comparative perspective*, Aldershot: Ashgate

Andreß, H.J. and Lipsmeir, G. (1995) 'Was gehört zum notwendigen Lebensstandard und wer kann ihn sich leisten? Ein neues Konzept zur Armutsmessung', *Aus Politik und Zeitgeschichte, Beilage zur Wochenzeitung Das Parlament*, B, 31-32/95 (28 July)

Atkinson, A.B. (1998) *Poverty in Europe*, Oxford: Blackwell

Atkinson, A.B., Rainwater, L. and Smeeding, T. (1995) 'Income distribution in OECD countries', *Social Policy Studies* 18, Paris: OECD

Beveridge, W. (1942) *Social insurance and allied services*, London: HM Stationery Office

Blair, T. (1999) 'Beveridge revisited: A welfare state for the twenty-first century', in R. Walker (ed.) *Ending child poverty*, Bristol: The Policy Press

Bradbury, B. (1989) 'Family size equivalence scales and survey evaluations of income and well-being', *Journal of Social Policy* 18(3): 383-408

Bradbury, B. and Jantii, M. (1999) *Child poverty across industrialised nations*, Innocenti Occasional Papers, EPS 1971, Florence: UNICEF

Bradshaw, J. (ed.) (1993) *Budget Standards for the United Kingdom*, Avebury: Aldershot

Bradshaw, J. (1999) 'Child poverty in comparative perspective', *European Journal of Social Security*, Volume 1, 4, 383-404

Bradshaw, J., Gordon, D., Levitas, R., Middleton, S., Pantazis, C., Payne, S. and Townsend, P. (1998) *Perceptions of poverty and social exclusion 1998*, Report on Preparatory Research, Bristol: Townsend Centre for International Poverty Research

Burns, D. (1992) *Poll tax rebellion*, Stirling: AK Press

Callan, T. and Nolan, B. (1991) 'Concepts of poverty and the poverty line', *Journal of Economic Surveys* 5(3): 243-61

Callan, T., Nolan, B. and Whelan, C.T. (1993) 'Resources, deprivation and the measurement of poverty', *Journal of Social Policy* 22(2): 141-72

Callan, T., Nolan, B., Whelan, B.J., Hannan, D.F. and Creighton, S. (1989) *Poverty, income and welfare in Ireland*, Dublin: Economic and Social Research Institute

Citro, C.F. and Michael, R.T. (eds) (1995) *Measuring poverty: A new approach*, Washington DC: National Academy Press

Cmd 4045 (1998) *Bringing Britain together: A national strategy for neighbourhood renewal*, Social Exclusion Unit, London: The Stationery Office

Colasanto, D., Kapteyn, A. and van der Gaag, J. (1984) 'Two subjective definitions of poverty: Results from the Wisconsin basic needs study', *Journal of Human Resources* 19(1): 127-38

Cornia, G.A. (1999) *Liberalisation, globalisation and income distribution*, Working Paper No. 157, Helsinki, Finland: UN World Institute for Development Economic Research

CSO (Central Statistical Office) (1996-9) *Family Expenditure Survey reports for 1996/7, 1997/8 and 1998/9*, London: The Stationery Office

Danziger, S., van der Gaag J., Taussig, M.K. and Smolensky, E. (1984) 'The direct measure of welfare levels: How much does it cost to make ends meet?', *Review of Economics and Statistics* 6(3): 500-05

Davey Smith, G. and Gordon, D. (1999) 'Poverty and health inequalities', in C. Pantazis and D. Gordon (eds) *Tackling inequalities: Where are we now and what can be done?*, Bristol: The Policy Press

Davey Smith, G. and Gordon, D. (2000) 'Poverty across the life-course and health', in Pantazis, C. and Gordon, D. (eds) *Tackling inequalities: where are we now and what can be done?* Bristol: The Policy Press, pp141-158

Davies, R. and Smith, W. (1998) *The basic necessities survey: The experience of Action Aid Vietnam*, London: Action Aid

Deleeck, H., de Lathouwer, L. and van den Bosch, K. (1988) *Social indicators of social security: A comparative analysis of five countries*, Antwerp: Centre for Social Policy

Deleeck, H., van den Bosch, K. and de Lathouwer, L. (eds) (1992) *Poverty and the adequacy of social security in the EC*, EUROPASS Research Consortium, Aldershot: Avebury

DETR (1998) *English House Conditions Survey: 1996*, London: DETR

Dobson, B. and Middleton, S. (1998) *Paying to care: The cost of childhood disability*, York: YPS/Joseph Rowntree Foundation

Drever, F., Fisher, K., Brown, J. and Clark, J. (2000) *Social inequalities: 2000 edition*, London: The Stationery Office

DSS (Department of Social Security) (1999a) *Households below average income 1994/5–1997/8*, London: Corporate Document Services

DSS (Department of Social Security) (1999b) *Opportunities for all: Tackling poverty and social exclusion*, Cmd 4445, London: The Stationery Office

DSS (Department of Social Security) (2000) *Households below average income 1998/9*, London: Corporate Document Services

EEC (1981) *Final report from the Commission to the Council on the first programme of pilot schemes and studies to combat poverty*, Brussels: Commission of the European Communities

EEC (1985) *On specific community action to combat poverty* (Council Decision of 19 December 1984) 85/8/EEC, Official Journal of the EEC, 2/24

Eurostat (1999) *European Community Household Panel (ECHP): Selected indicators from the 1995 wave*, Luxembourg: Office for Official Publications of the EC

Goedhart, T., Halberstadt, V., Kapteyn, A. and Van Praag, B. (1977) 'The poverty line: concept and measurement', *Journal of Human Resources* 12(4): 503-20

Goode, J., Callender, C. and Lister, R. (1998) *Purse or wallet? Gender inequalities and income distribution within families on benefits*, London: Policy Studies Institute

Gordon, D. (1995) 'Census based deprivation indices: Their weighting and validation', *Journal of Epidemiology and Community Health*, 49 (Suppl 2), S39-S44

Gordon, D. (2000) 'Inequalities in income, wealth and standard of living', in C. Pantazis and D. Gordon (eds) *Tackling inequalities: Where are we now and what can be done?* Bristol: The Policy Press

Gordon, D., Davey Smith, G., Dorling, D. and Shaw, M. (eds) (1999) *Inequalities in health: The evidence presented to the Independent Inquiry into Inequalities in Health*, Bristol: The Policy Press

Gordon, D. and Pantazis, C. (1997) *Breadline Britain in the 1990s*, Ashgate: Aldershot

Gordon, D., Parker, R and Loughran, F. with Heslop, P. (2000) *Disabled children in Britain: A reanalysis of the OPCS Disability Surveys*, London: The Stationery Office

Gordon, D. and Spicker, P. (eds) (1999) *The international glossary on poverty*, Cape Town, Dhaka, Bangkok, London and New York: Zed Books

Gordon, D. and Townsend, P. (1990) 'Measuring the poverty line', *Radical Statistics*, 47, 5-12

Gore, C. and Figueiredo, J.B. (1996) *Social exclusion and anti-poverty strategies*, Geneva: International Institute for Labour Studies

GSS (1998) *Harmonised Concepts and Questions for Government Social Surveys*, London: Government Statistical Service

Hagenaars, A.J.M. (1986) *The perceptions of poverty*, Amsterdam: Elsevier Science Publishers

Hagenaars, A.J.M. and de Vos, K. (1988) 'The definition and measurement of poverty', *Journal of Human Resources* 23(2): 211-21

Halleröd, B. (1994) *Poverty in Sweden: A new approach to direct measurement of consensual poverty*, Umeå Studies in Sociology, No. 10 6, University of Umeå

Halleröd, B. (1995a) 'Perceptions of poverty in Sweden', *Scandinavian Journal of Social Welfare* 4(3): 174-89

Halleröd, B. (1995b) 'The truly poor: indirect and direct measurement of consensual poverty in Sweden', *Journal of European Social Policy* 5(2): 111-29

Halleröd, B. (1998) 'Poor Swedes, poor Britons: A comparative analysis of relative deprivation', in H.J. Andreß (ed.) *Empirical poverty research in a comparative perspective*, Aldershot: Ashgate

Hills, J. (1995) *Income and wealth, volume 2: A summary of the evidence*, York: Joseph Rowntree Foundation

Hills, J. (ed.) (1996) *New inequalities: The changing distribution of income and wealth in the United Kingdom*, Cambridge: Cambridge University Press

Hills, J. (1998) *Income and wealth: The latest evidence*, York: Joseph Rowntree Foundation

HM Treasury (Nov 1999) 'Supporting children through the tax and benefit system', *The modernisation of Britain's tax and benefit system*, 5, London: The Stationery Office

HM Treasury (March 2000) 'Tackling poverty and making work pay – tax credits for the 21st Century', *The modernisation of Britain's tax and benefit system*, 6, London: The Stationery Office

Howarth, C., Kenway, P., Palmer, G. and Miorelli, R. (1999) *Monitoring poverty and social exclusion 1999*, York: Joseph Rowntree Foundation

Independent Inquiry into Inequalities in Health (1998) *Report of the Independent Inquiry into Inequalities in Health*, London: The Stationery Office

Kangas, O. and Ritakallio, V. (1995) *Different methods - different results? Approaches to multidimensional poverty*, Paper presented at the ISARC 19 Conference, Pavi, Italy

Kangas, O. and Ritakallio, V.M. (1998) 'Different methods – different results? Approaches to multidimensional poverty', in H.J. Andreß (ed.) *Empirical poverty research in a comparative perspective*, Aldershot: Ashgate

Levitas, R. (1999) *The inclusive society*, London: Macmillan

Mack, J. and Lansley, S. (1985) *Poor Britain*, London: Allen and Unwin

Marsh, A., Gordon, D., Pantazis, C. and Heslop, P. (1999) *Home, sweet home? The impact of poor housing on health*, Bristol: The Policy Press

Martin, J. and White, A. (1988) *The financial circumstances of adults living in private households*, Report 2, London: HMSO

Mayer, S.E. and Jencks, C. (1988) 'Poverty and the distribution of material hardship', *The Journal of Human Resources* XXIV.1: 88-113

Middleton, S., Ashworth, K. and Braithwaite, I. (1997) *Small fortunes: Spending on children, childhood poverty and parental sacrifice*, York: Joseph Rowntree Foundation

Middleton, S., Ashworth, K. and Walker, R. (1994) *Family fortunes: pressures on parents and children in the 1990s*, London: CPAG Ltd

Muffels, R. and Vries, A. de (1989) *Poverty in the Netherlands, first report of an international comparative study*, Tilburg: VUGA

Muffels, R., Kapteyn, A., Vries, A. de and Berghman, J. (1990), *Poverty in the Netherlands: Report on the Dutch Contribution to an International Comparative Study on Poverty and the Financial Efficacy of the Social Security System*, The Hague: VUGA

Muffels, R. and Vreins, M. (1991) 'The elaboration of a deprivation scale and the definition of a subjective deprivation poverty line', paper presented at the *Annual Meeting of the European Society for Population Economic*, 6-8 June, Pisa

Muffels, R., Berghman, J. and Dirven, H. (1992) 'A multi-method approach to monitor the evolution of poverty', *Journal of European Social Policy* 2(3): 193-213

Nolan, B.J. and Whelan, C.T. (1996a) *Resources, deprivation and poverty*, Oxford: Clarendon Press

Nolan, B.J. and Whelan, C.T. (1996b) 'Measuring poverty using income and deprivation indicators: alternative approaches', *Journal of European Social Policy* 6(3): 225-40

Nunnally, J.C. (1981) *Psychometric theory*, New Delhi: Tate McGraw-Hill Publishing Company Ltd

Nyman, C. (1996) 'Inside the black box: Intra-household distribution of consumption in Sweden', in E. Bihagen, C. Nyman and M. Strand (eds) *Three aspects of consensual poverty in Sweden - work deprivation, attitudes towards the welfare state and household consumptional distribution*, Umeå, Sweden: Umeå University

ONS (Office for National Statistics) (1998) *Social trends 28*, London: The Stationery Office

ONS (Office for National Statistics) (1999) *Social trends 29*, London: The Stationery Office

ONS (Office for National Statistics) (2000) *Social trends 30*, London: The Stationery Office

Orshansky, M. (1965) 'Counting the poor: another look at the poverty profile', *Social Security Bulletin*, June, 3-29

Payne, S. and Pantazis, C. (1997) 'Poverty and gender', in D. Gordon and C. Pantazis (eds) *Breadline Britain in the 1990s*, Aldershot: Ashgate

Piachaud, D. and Sutherland, H. (2000) *How effective is the British Government's attempt to reduce child poverty?*, CASE paper 38, London: Centre for Analysis of Social Exclusion, LSE

Ramprakash, D. (1994) 'Poverty in the countries of the European Union: A synthesis of Eurostat's research on poverty', *Journal of European Social Policy*, 4(2): 117-28

Reynolds, M. (1992) *Uncollectable: the story of the poll tax revolt*, Manchester: Greater Manchester Anti-Poll Tax Federation

Room, G. (ed.) (1995) *Beyond the threshold: the measurement and analysis of social exclusion*, Bristol: The Policy Press

Rowntree, B.S. (1901) *Poverty: A study of town life*, London: Macmillan & Co.

Rowntree, B.S. (1941) *Poverty and progress: A second social survey of York*, London: Longmans, Green & Co.

Rowntree, B.S. and Lavers, G.R. (1951) *Poverty and the welfare state: A third social survey of York dealing only with economic questions*, London: Longmans, Green & Co.

Rubinstein, W.D. (1986) *Wealth and inequality in Britain*, London: Faber and Faber

Saltow, L. (1968) 'Long run changes in British income inequality', *Economic History Review*, 2nd Series: 21

Saunders, P. and Matheson, G. (1992) *Perceptions of poverty, income adequacy and living standards in Australia*, Social Policy Research Centre, Sydney: University of New South Wales (Reports and Proceedings No 99)

Scottish Homes (1997) *Scottish House Conditions Survey*, Edinburgh: Scottish Homes

Shaw, M., Dorling, D., Gordon, D. and Davey Smith, G. (1999) *The widening gap: Health inequalities and policy in Britain*, Bristol: The Policy Press

Silver, H. (1994) 'Social exclusion and social solidarity: Three paradigms', *International Labour Review*, Vol. 133, No. 5-6

Smyth, M. and Robus, N. (1989) *The financial circumstances of families with disabled children living in private households*, OPCS Surveys of Disability Report 5, London: HMSO

Szalai, J. (ed.) (1998) 'Old and new poverty in post-1989 Central Europe', special issue of *East-Central Europe*, Vol. 20-23, parts 3-4

Townsend, P. (1962) 'The meaning of poverty', *British Journal of Sociology* 8

Townsend, P. (ed.) (1970) *The concept of poverty*, London: Heinemann

Townsend, P. (1979) *Poverty in the United Kingdom*, London: Allen Lane and Penguin Books

Townsend, P. (1993) *The international analysis of poverty*, Hemel Hempstead: Harvester Wheatsheaf

Townsend, P. and Davidson, N. (1988) *Inequalities in health: The Black Report*, 2nd edition, London: Penguin Books

Townsend, P. and Gordon, D. (1989) 'What is enough?' in House of Commons Social Services Committee, *Minimum Income*, House of Commons 579, HMSO: London

Townsend, P. and Gordon, D. (1991) 'What is enough? New evidence on poverty allowing the definition of a minimum benefit', in M. Alder, C. Bell, J. Clasen and A. Sinfield (eds) *The Sociology of Social Security*, Edinburgh: Edinburgh University Press, pp35-69

Townsend, P., Gordon, D., Bradshaw, J. and Gosschalk, B. (1997) *Absolute and overall poverty in Britain in 1997: What the population themselves say*, Report of the Second MORI Survey, University of Bristol: Bristol Statistical Monitoring Unit

Townsend, P., Gordon, D. and Gosschalk, B. (1996) 'The poverty line in Britain today: What the population themselves say', *Statistical Monitoring Unit Report No. 7*, University of Bristol

UN (1995) *The Copenhagen declaration and programme of action: World summit for social development 6-12 March 1995*, New York: United Nations Department of Publications

UNDP (1997) *Human development report 1997*, New York and Oxford: Oxford University Press

UNDP (1998) *Poverty in transition*, Regional Bureau for Europe and the CIS, New York: UNDP

UNICEF (2000) *A league table of child poverty in rich nations, Innocenti Report Card Issue No.1*, Florence: UNICEF Innocenti Research Centre

Van den Bosch, K. (1998) 'Perceptions of the minimum standard of living in Belgium: Is there a consensus?', in H.J. Andreß (ed.) *Empirical poverty research in a comparative perspective*, Aldershot: Ashgate

Van Praag, B., Hagenaars, A. and van Weeren J. (1980) *Poverty in Europe*, Report to the Commission of the EC, University of Leyden

Veit-Wilson, J.H. (1987) 'Consensual approaches to poverty lines and social security', *Journal of Social Policy* 16(2): 183-211

Vogel, J. (1997) *Living conditions and inequality in the European Union 1997*, Eurostat Working Papers: Population and Social Conditions E/1997-3, Luxembourg: Eurostat

Walker, R. (1987) 'Consensual approaches to the definition of poverty: Towards an alternative methodology', *Journal of Social Policy* 16(2): 213-26

Wedgwood, J. (1929) *The economics of inheritance*, Harmondsworth: Penguin

Whitehead, M. (1988) *Inequalities in health: The health divide*, 2nd edition, London: Penguin Books

World Bank (1990) *World Development Report 1990: Poverty*, Washington DC: World Bank

World Bank (1996) *Poverty reduction and the World Bank: Progress and challenges in the 1990s*, Washington DC: World Bank

WHO (1998) *The World Health Report 1998: Life in the 21st century: A vision for all*, Geneva: WHO

Zarb, G. and Maher, L. (1997) *The financial circumstances of disabled people in Northern Ireland*, PPRU Surveys of Disability Report No. 6, Belfast: NISRA